Written by Alison Baker
for and on behalf of the
Seaford Head Local Nature Reserve
Management Committee

October 2018

Published by Country Books/Ashridge Press
in association with Spiral Publishing Ltd

Country Books Courtyard Cottage, Little Longstone,
Bakewell, Derbyshire DE45 1NN

Tel: 01629 640670
email: dickrichardson@countrybooks.biz

www.countrybooks.biz
www.sussexbooks.co.uk

ISBN 978-1-910489-74-1

© 2019 Alison Baker

The rights Country Books for this edition have been asserted in accordance with the Copyright, Designs and Patents Act 1993.

All rights reserved. No part of this publication may be reproduced, stored in a retrieval system, or transmitted, in any way or form, or by any means, electronic, mechanical, photocopying, or otherwise, without the prior permission of the author and publisher.

British Library Cataloguing in Publication Data.
A catalogue record for this book is available from the British Library.

Printed and bound in by Print2Demand Ltd,
1 Newlands Road, Westoning, Bedfordshire, MK45 5LD

~ Contents ~

Timeline	6
Acknowledgements	8
Introduction	9
Land Acquisition	10
LNR establishment and extensions	15
Governance	19
Land Management	28
Dewpond	45
Dog Fouling	50
Harry's Bush	52
Hope Gap Steps	54
Promotion and publicity	59
Interpretation Boards	62
Open Days	65
Rabbits	66
Saline Lagoon	68
Surveys	73

Miscellaneous:

Artichoke Peace Camp	86
Canadian War Memorial	87
Civil Aviation Navigation Beacon	90
Country Club Proposal	94
Drones	95
Filming	96
Foreshore	98
Oil Pollution	102
One-offs – Unexpected Treasure	104
The Future	108

Appendices:

Appendix 1 – SHLNRMC Chairs	110
Appendix 2 – Wardens/Rangers	110
Appendix 3 – Filming	111
Appendix 4 – Species unique to Seaford Head among the 33 SWT-managed Nature Reserves	112
Bibliography	115
Glossary	116
Index	118

~ Timeline ~

1887 — 12-hole Golf Links laid out by Thompson of Felixstowe.
1889 — Golf course extended to 18 holes.
1914 — Part of World War 1 South Camp of Kitchener's Third New Army.
1928 — Purchase by Seaford Urban District Council of 200 acres (81Ha) of land on Seaford Head, including the Golf Links.
1933 — Purchase of an additional 357 acres (144Ha) by Seaford Urban District Council from the estate of the late Hugh Hamilton Stafford Northcote.
1940 — World War 2 Anti-aircraft gun emplacement and invasion defences established. Golf course ploughed up for food production.
1953 — Site of Special Scientific Interest (SSSI) designation of part of the current site.
1960 — Aircraft navigation beacon (VOR) sited on Seaford Head by order of the Secretary of State on behalf of the Civil Aviation Authority.
1966 — Seaford Urban District Council agree in principle to 90 acres of downland becoming a Local Nature Reserve (LNR).
1966 — Designation as South Downs Area of Outstanding Natural Beauty (AONB). (This was revoked in 2010 due to the imminent establishment of the South Downs National Park).
1968 — Committee of 4 persons convened to press for land at Seaford Head to become a Local Nature Reserve.
1969 — Becomes a Local Nature Reserve of 76 acres designated under the National Parks and Access to the Countryside Act 1949.
1971 — First Constitution and Terms of Reference agreed for Seaford Head Local Nature Reserve Management Committee (SHLNRMC).
1973 — Sussex Heritage Coast designation
1974 — Local Government re-organisation results in the land being transferred to Lewes District Council
1974 — Mr A (John) Gascoigne appointed first Honorary Warden (part-time)
1976 — Eastern extension approved (LNR now 193 acres).
1978 — Western extension and foreshore added (LNR now 244 acres)
1978 — First Guide Leaflet produced. 1000 copies in green text on cream paper printed.
1979 — Second edition of Guide Leaflet produced, to include western extension and foreshore, reprinted in February and again in June 1981.

~ Timeline ~

1980 — Official opening of steps to the foreshore at Hope Gap.
1980 — First detailed Management Plan adopted.
1981 — Retirement of Mr R (Bob) Batchelor, Sussex Ornithological Society representative and Committee Member since 1969.
1983 — Founder member Mr H J Harrison retires from Committee (he had also served as Secretary for 6 years).
1985 — Extension of SSSI to include the whole of the Local Nature Reserve and land along the Cuckmere valley.
1986 — Death of Mr J (Jack) Harrison, Sussex Naturalists Trust representative and founder member of the Committee.
1986 — Designation of the South Downs (including Seaford Head) as an (ESA) Environmentally Sensitive Area.
1987 — Designation as Voluntary Marine Conservation Area.
1987 — Conversion of civil aviation beacon from VOR to DVOR.
1989 — Harry's Bush extension to the Local Nature Reserve approved.
1992 — Death of Mr G (Chris) Hemingway, Management Committee founder and member for 23 years. Seaford Natural History Society representative.
1993 — Chyngton Farm Estate 284 acres (119 Ha) purchased by National Trust
1993 — 42 acres between the meanders and the new cut in the Cuckmere valley purchased by East Sussex County Council.
1999 — Seaford Town Council established.
2005 — Ownership of land on Seaford Head transferred to Seaford Town Council from Lewes District Council
2006 — Erection and dedication of Canadian War Memorial
2011 — Reserve becomes part of the South Downs National Park (SDNP) established on 1st April.
2013 — Management of the Reserve taken on by Sussex Wildlife Trust (SWT). Management plan (2013-2017) compiled and approved.
2014 — Current condition of the SSSI assessed by Natural England and listed as "recovering but not yet favourable."
2017 — 25 year lease granted to Sussex Wildlife Trust to manage the Local Nature Reserve.
2019 — Fiftieth Anniversary of Local Nature Reserve Status.

~ Acknowledgements ~

I would like to thank the following for their help in the production of this booklet:

My husband, Paul Baker, who has helped with the research and cast a critical eye over my text producing a much better result than would otherwise have been the case;

Georgia Raeburn, the Seaford Town Council and archives;

Paul Waller, the Seaford Museum & Heritage Society members and archives;

Kevin Gordon, Seaford historian

Seaford Natural History Society members and archives;

Seaford Head Local Nature Reserve Management Committee members and archives;

Sussex Wildlife Trust;

Lewes District Council;

The Crown Estates;

David Paul;

Dave Morgan, the National Trust and archives;

Staff at The Keep in Brighton;

And last but not least, Anne Fletcher, who was responsible for involving me in this project!

All materials researched in the production of this booklet are listed in the bibliography but the interpretation of evidence, as well as any errors and omissions are all my own.

~ Introduction ~

Introduction

I was asked by the Seaford Head Local Nature Reserve Management Committee, whose Chairman is Chris Lowmass, to compile a history of the Local Nature Reserve in time for its 50th anniversary on 1st February 2019.

My background is as a local historian, so I am indebted to my husband Paul for ensuring I don't get engrossed in the history of the site and lose the *natural* history focus.

But where to start? With the formation of the Local Nature Reserve? But that didn't just happen, there was something there before. I needed to start with the land, how did it come to be in public ownership? And by what mechanism did it become a Nature Reserve?

What information was out there? Where was it? How complete was it going to be? How easy was it going to be to access? I needn't have worried; in fact there was so much that I eventually had to call a halt to the research and start writing if I was to meet the deadline. You can see from the bibliography that there were plenty of records from a wide variety of sources including talking to the people who were there.

This text is my findings to date, some of which may turn out to need radical revision – please feel free to point out any errors or, indeed, add anything you can to the information already acquired.

1969 was a momentous year. Man walked on the Moon for the first time, the iconic Woodstock pop festival was held, the Beatles released their equally iconic Abbey Road album and, not to be outdone, Seaford Head became a Local Nature Reserve!

Declared a Site of Special Scientific Interest (SSSI) in 1953 as part of the Seaford to Beachy Head designation, this popular and much used site is also part of the Sussex Downs National Park and the Sussex Heritage Coast. It is a Site of Nature Conservation Importance, a Local Geological Site, a Regionally Important Geomorphological Site and was declared a Voluntary Marine Conservation Area in 1987. The Vanguard Way long distance footpath passes through on its way from Newhaven to Croydon.

2019 marks the fiftieth anniversary of this jewel in Seaford's crown and this text sets out to document and celebrate those first 50 years.

~ Land Acquisition ~

Land Acquisition

By the late 1890's most of Seaford was owned by two major landholders – the Pelham's, family name of the Earls of Chichester, who owned the 1,026 acre Chyngton Estate and the Harison's who owned the 857 acre Sutton Estate.

The 1898 edition of Kelly's Directory contained a list of *"old family names at present in Seaford"* and this shows that the Harison's were recorded in the town as early as 1657, and latterly lived in Sutton Place, now part of the recently closed Newlands School. By 1897 the Sutton Estate had passed to Launcelot Harison, (yes, both spellings are correct; hence Harison Road on what was part of the Sutton Estate). Mr Harison was listed in the 1901 census as being 46 years old, blind, a widower, and living in Acton with his sister and brother-in-law. This is probably the reason why he had not lived in Seaford for some time and was prepared to sell the family Estate.

Town Seal of Seaford
- *Image courtesy of David Paul*

The town wanted to capitalise on the growing popularity of Brighton and Eastbourne as holiday destinations and the golf course had been established in 1887 primarily to provide something to do for all the people who were going to flock to the resort of Seaford. There was a lot of development happening at the time on, and around, the seafront to attract and accommodate these eagerly anticipated tourists.

The original golf course had consisted of 12 holes, with two more being added in 1895 and the final four holes in 1899. A separate 9-hole course for the ladies section was constructed in 1895 alongside the men's course. The inadequate facilities at the golf clubhouse and a wish to improve these led to an attempt to

~ Land Acquisition ~

purchase the freehold of the course. The new owner, however, had other ideas for the land and this led to a split within the Club with some members forming a new golf club on land in Blatchington and the remainder playing on at the renamed Seaford Head Golf Course.

The new owner was Alfred Blandford Hutchings and he had purchased the whole of the Sutton Estate which included the golf course and clubhouse in April 1897. Mr Hutchings is an interesting character: born in Grimsby in 1851 but raised in London, he moved to Seaford in the early 1900's to go into the property development business. He describes himself as an architect in the 1891 census, living at that time in Lewisham, but already very involved with the Seaford Golf Club. When he purchased the Sutton Estate he moved his family into Sutton Place and, with his son Alan, set about realising his plans for development. But the gamble didn't pay off and 800 acres of the Sutton Estate, including the golf course, went up for sale again in May 1906. Apparently none of the lots met their reserve price and none were sold that day. Presumably in an attempt to attract new investment his company was renamed Sutton Park Ltd and despite mortgaging and re-mortgaging he finally went bankrupt in 1924. By this time he had constructed quite a lot of buildings, particularly private schools, in Seaford and his trademark of a property with a corner turret can still be seen in many houses around the town.

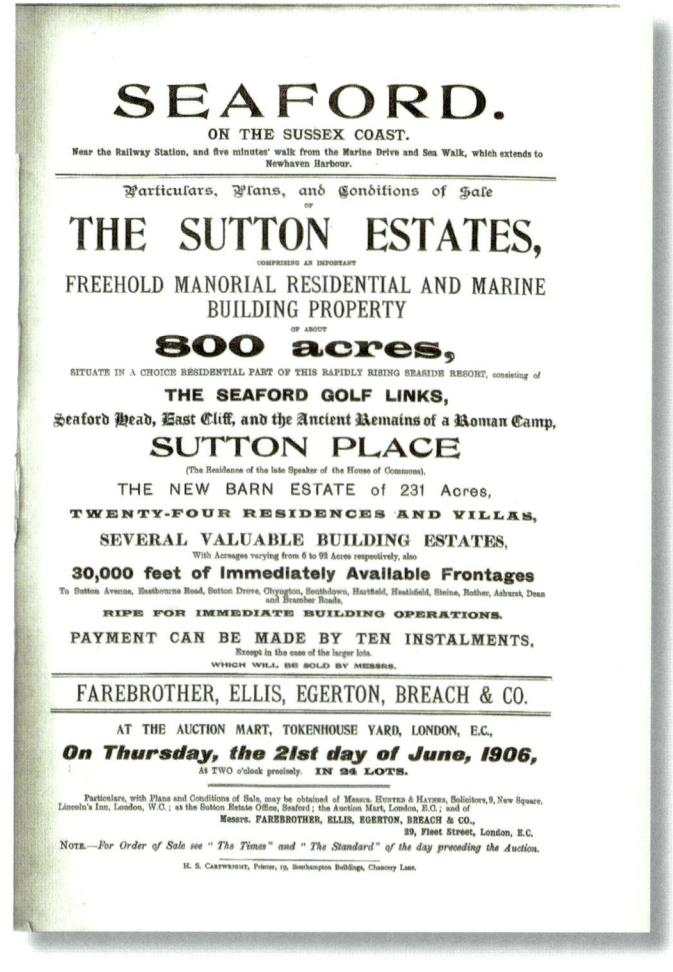

Auction Poster 1906
- Image courtesy of Seaford Museum and Heritage Society

~ *Land Acquisition* ~

The land was sold piecemeal to meet debts, presumably starting with the more attractive lots since it was 1926 before Seaford Urban District Council entered the frame as a prospective buyer. It was obviously a complicated transaction since the Seaford Head Estate (as the deal was called), consisted of 9 lots, each one having Mr Hutchings and at least one other interested party on the deeds. Negotiations dragged on until Feb 1927 when it was reported that a local house agent had received instructions to auction the golf clubhouse, and another firm had been asked to divide the golf links into building plots. Whether this was a ploy on behalf of Hutchings' creditors to move things along or not we will never know, but maybe that's how close the golf links came to disappearing under bricks and concrete.

In November 1927 The Times newspaper reported that there was *"slight opposition to the scheme on account of increasing the local rates, but the whole matter will come before a town meeting tomorrow evening".* Although there are some references in the Urban District Council Minutes to holding a public meeting I can find no written evidence that it ever took place, nor any evidence that the local rates were increased to pay back the loan, although this is extremely likely.

Finally, according to the same Urban District Council Minutes, 200 acres (including the golf course and clubhouse) were purchased on 21st May 1928 for £16,527 to preserve the area for the public as an open space. This included land to the west of Southdown Road, later sold by Lewes District Council for housing. The cheque for this purchase is on display in the Seaford Martello Tower Local History Museum. Councillor James Hooper, JP (1862-1938), a tailor with premises in Church Street, who was elected onto the newly established Seaford Urban District Council in 1894 (and remained a Councillor for 35 years), *"was*

SEAFORD HEAD.

PROPOSED PURCHASE FOR THE PUBLIC.

(FROM OUR CORRESPONDENT.)

SEAFORD, Nov. 15.

Subject to the Ministry of Health's consent, Seaford Urban Council has decided, after long negotiations, to purchase Seaford Head for the sum of £16,500 to preserve the area for the public as an open space. The land, which includes an 18-hole golf course and club house, is about 200 acres in extent. If the land is purchased the downs will be open from Seaford to Eastbourne and will constitute the finest stretch of seaboard on the South Coast. The links will be run as a municipal concern.

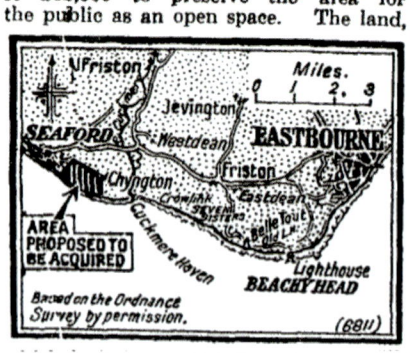

There is slight opposition to the scheme on account of increasing the local rates, but the whole matter will come before a town meeting to-morrow evening. The Council hopes that financial help will be forthcoming from those interested in the downs.

The Times, Nov. 1927

~ Land Acquisition ~

always proud that he was one of the signatories to the cheque which purchased the Seaford Head and golf links".

Meanwhile, also in 1927, the Chyngton Estate of the Earls of Chichester came on the market having been in the family for 400 years. The 6th Earl of Chichester, Jocelyn Brudenell Pelham and his 21 year old heir Francis Godolphin Henry Pelham had succumbed to pneumonia within days of each other and the land was being sold to meet the double death duties.

It was purchased by Hugh Hamilton Stafford Northcote, *"for the purpose of preserving intact the rural beauty of the cliffs on that (western) side of the valley"*. He moved into Chyngton House and initiated negotiations with the Urban District Council, the National Trust (who had recently purchased the Crowlink Estate) and the owners of the Exceat Estate to protect and preserve the whole of the coastline between Seaford Head and Beachy Head, but unfortunately died in January 1929 before agreement had been reached.

This local philanthropist left instructions in his will that the portion of the Chyngton Estate on Seaford Head, consisting of 357 acres, should be sold to the Urban District Council for the nominal fee of £250 to ensure *"that the whole of Seaford Head will be preserved for the public in future"* and this sale was completed in 1933.

The Seaford Urban District Council landholding was now 557 acres and to manage some of this an agricultural tenancy, the South Hill Farm, was created on 274 acres. It is still in existence and the evidence can be seen on each side of the access road and in the fields around South Hill Barn.

Chyngton Farmhouse and the adjoining 284 acres were tenanted by Mr Daniel Paul from 1927. Mr Paul is listed as occupying this portion of the old Chichester Estate in the 1932 Sale Particulars. Mr Paul purchased the land in 1950 from the Seaford Downs Estate and in 1993 the farm was purchased from his company, DL Paul & Sons Ltd, by the National Trust;

GENERAL VIEW OF THE RESIDENCE & FARMBUILDINGS & BUILDING.

Chyngton Estate 1932 - *image courtesy of David Paul*

~ Land Acquisition ~

the purchase being financed by the National Trusts South Downs Appeal, the Countryside Commission and a bequest by Mr R L How. This farm is once again the subject of an agricultural tenancy and the land is being managed on behalf of the National Trust.

Ownership of the Seaford Head Estate passed to Lewes District Council in 1974 following the demise of Seaford Urban District Council as part of the Local Government Reform Act 1974 and was not handed back to the newly formed (1999) Seaford Town Council until 2005.

In 1993 East Sussex County Council purchased the 42 acres between the meanders and the New Cut (the Brooklands) on the eastern side of the Cuckmere Valley, seaward of the Exceat causeway, from the Paul family to extend the Seven Sisters Country Park and thus the current landowners of the Local Nature Reserve was complete (see 1994 map below).

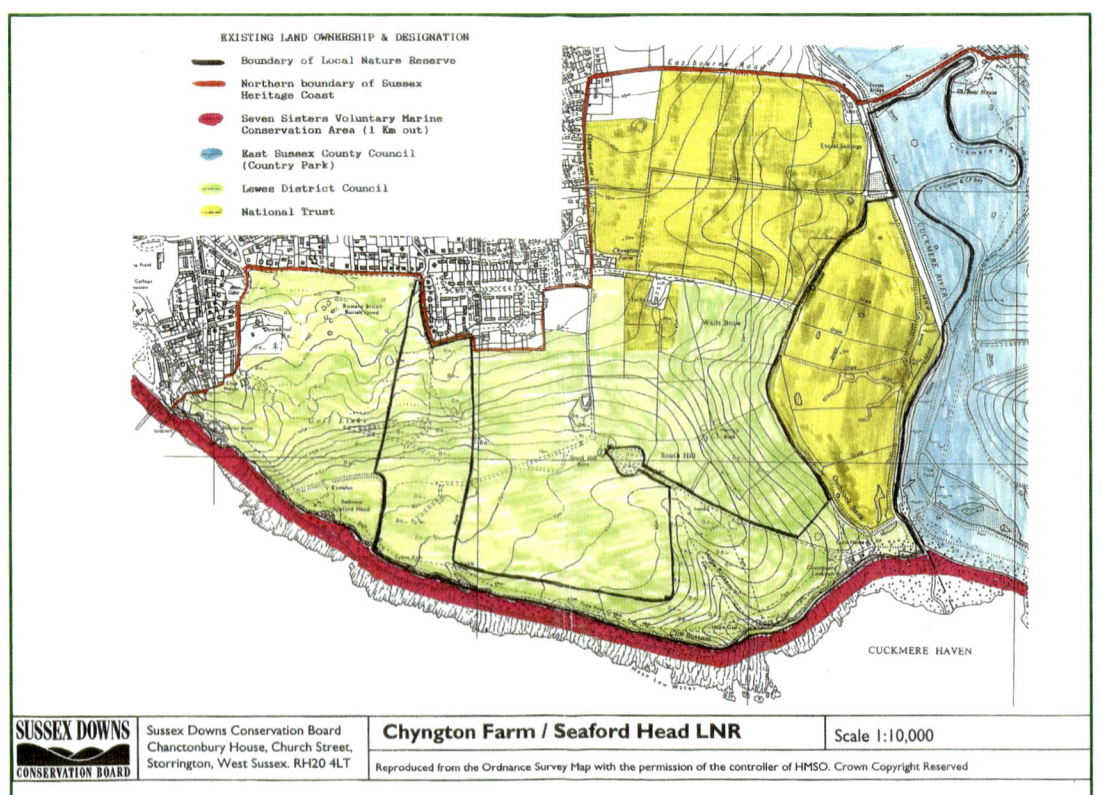

1994 Map showing land ownership on Seaford Head.
Lewes District Council's (now Seaford Town Council) landholding is coloured green, National Trust in yellow and East Sussex County Council in blue. Black line denotes LNR boundary.

~ Establishment of a Local Nature Reserve ~

Establishment of a Local Nature Reserve

In 1953 part of Seaford Head was designated a Site of Special Scientific Interest (SSSI) under Section 28 of the National Parks and Access to the Countryside Act 1949 by The Nature Conservancy who were the Government body tasked with implementing this legislation. The purpose of the 1949 Act was to allow people to *"…….derive great pleasure from the peaceful contemplation of nature."* There is no record as to exactly why Seaford Head was originally chosen but it is now the most important area in Sussex for several rare species, including the Moon Carrot and the Potter Flower-bee, perhaps these or other rare species were known to be in the Reserve back then too. It is important to note that this landscape was already recognised as distinctive 16 years before the creation of the Local Nature Reserve (LNR).

A report formally requesting the formation of a Local Nature Reserve, probably authored by Mr Chris Hemingway (a founder member of the Natural History Society and a teacher at Blatchington Court School) stated in 1966 that, *"from a botanical point of view, the coastal area extending from Seaford Head to Cuckmere Haven and the River Cuckmere inland as far as Exceat Bridge is notable not only for the number of uncommon species which are found there but also for its wide variety of contrasting and relatively undisturbed habitats. As such, it is not only one of the most attractive and unspoilt parts of the Sussex coast but of very great interest to lovers of wild flowers and students of the British flora and a convenient locality to which students and school-children may be taken to learn about a wide range of vegetation types."* Attached to this report was a list of over 220 botanical species recorded as being present in this area.

Hope Gap - *Photo by Alison Baker*

~ Establishment of a Local Nature Reserve ~

In a letter supporting this application Mr Martin Port of Brighton, who had clearly been bird watching on Seaford Head for some years, said in October 1966, *"the chief merit of the place, however, is that .... this is the only sizeable area of bush providing shelter for [bird] migrants left on the coast between Eastbourne and Newhaven. There are many elder bushes and brambles, the cover is thick and no doubt insect life is plentiful. All the common migrants shelter and feed in the bushes or on the grassland in the valley in good quantity."*

Later that same year Seaford Urban District Council, acknowledging the case for conservation, agreed in principle to 90 acres becoming a Local Nature Reserve, and in 1968 a committee of four people convened to press The Nature Conservancy to declare this: Mr Hemingway – see above; Mr Harrison – representing Sussex Naturalists Trust, now Sussex Wildlife Trust, (and also a Natural History Society member); Mr Harvey – representing The Nature Conservancy, now Natural England; and Councillor Myers of Seaford Urban District Council.

Their submission was clearly successful as a Local Nature Reserve of 76 acres was established on Seaford Head on 1st February 1969 and the Seaford Head Local Nature Reserve Management Committee (SHLNRMC) was formed later the same year. There is no record of what happened to prune the 90 acres being talked about in 1966.

Cuckmere Valley - *Photo by Alison Baker*

The extent of the original Local Nature Reserve is shown on the map on page 18 in red (South Hill Barn is by the small red, teardrop, shaped patch). Almost immediately negotiations commenced for an extension to the east (on land owned by D L Paul & Sons Ltd), shown in green on the map, and this was approved in 1976. The Local Nature Reserve was now 193 acres. Having achieved this, attention turned to providing a western extension (including the foreshore between high and low water levels), [see separate section on the Foreshore], shown in blue on the map. This was approved in 1978, increasing the Local Nature Reserve to 244 acres.

~ Establishment of a Local Nature Reserve ~

In an article written by Mr Harrison in 1971 for The Seaford Naturalist, the newsletter of the Seaford Natural History Society it was reported that *"the whole of the Cuckmere Estuary, together with Seaford Head and the Seven Sisters, are included in one Site of Special Scientific Interest described by the Nature Conservancy as 'an area of exceptional interest including chalk marshes and chalk cliffs, all having a rich and characteristic flora including a number of rare plants. The bird population is also of interest'."* They must have retained their interest in the site because in 1985 the Nature Conservancy Council, (Nature Conservancy was renamed in 1973), extended the SSSI to include the whole of the Local Nature Reserve and the land along the Cuckmere Valley.

By 1988 attention had turned to the possible inclusion of Harry's Bush into the Reserve. A site meeting was held to consider the proposal and it was agreed that, *"although it was bounded by agricultural land and wouldn't be generally available to the public, Harry's Bush would be an important and valuable addition to the Reserve because: the whole area provides a useful nesting and roosting site for a number of bird species; it would facilitate management to enhance its nature conservation interest with recent fencing encouraging the growth of a valuable herb and shrub layer; the woodland habitat is not present in the rest of the Reserve, thereby adding diversity and interest; and the grazed pasture habitat type is not represented in the rest of the Reserve and will be a useful addition."* [See separate section on Harry's Bush].

Harry's Bush - *Photo by Alison Baker*

Accordingly Lewes District Council, who had acquired all the assets when the Seaford Urban District Council was disbanded in 1974, were requested to apply to have this land declared to be managed as a nature reserve under Section 21(i) of the National Parks and Access to the Countryside Act 1949. In September 1989 it was reported that this land, shown in orange/brown on the map, had now been officially adopted as part of the Reserve. Thus the boundaries of the Local Nature Reserve were complete and have remained unchanged ever since.

~ *Establishment of a Local Nature Reserve* ~

Key to Map:

Red = original Local Nature Reserve [1969]

Green = eastern extension [1976]

Blue = western extension, clearly showing the foreshore as part of the Reserve [1978]

Orange/Brown = Harrys Bush [1989]

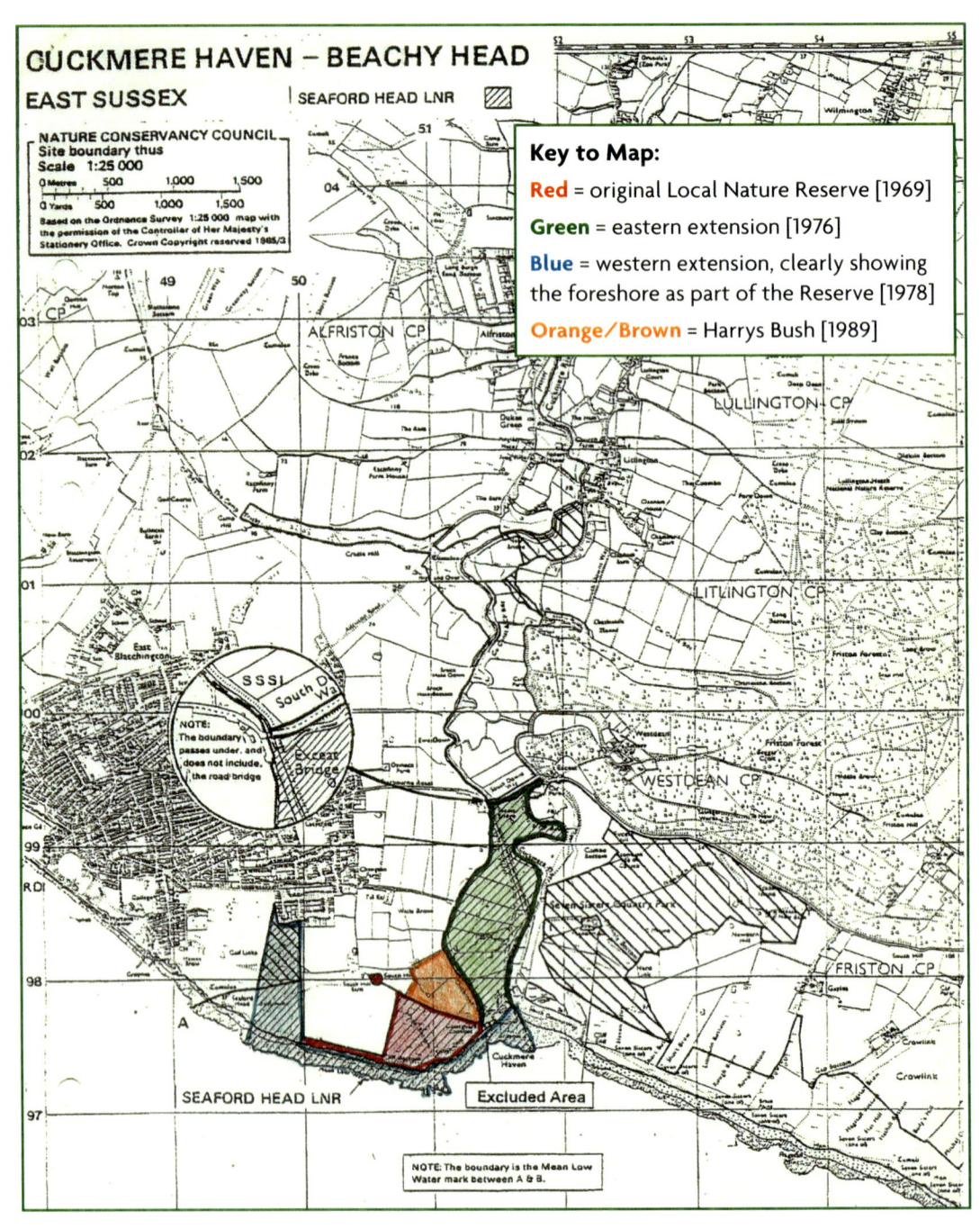

1985 Nature Conservancy Council SSSI designation map overlaid with the original Local Nature Reserve plus boundary extensions. Note: the Harry's Bush extension (marked in orange) is the only part of the LNR not in the SSSI.

(N.B. The 'excluded area' referred to on the map are the Coastguard Cottages and gardens which are not part of the Reserve.) Image from Seaford Town Council archives.

~ Governance ~

Governance

As explained in the first section, at the time of the inauguration of Seaford Head as a Local Nature Reserve in 1969 the land was owned by the Seaford Urban District Council (SUDC). The Management Committee which was formed to oversee and manage the Reserve consisted of representatives from the Seaford Natural History Society, Sussex Naturalists Trust (now Sussex Wildlife Trust), Nature Conservancy (now Natural England) and was chaired by Councillor Vic Myers, a SUDC Councillor.

Seaford Head Local Nature Reserve Management Committee Logo

The first constitution was adopted in 1971 and allowed for the management of the whole of the Nature Reserve, including the proposed extension, with the number of Committee members being increased to seven members by the addition of a representative from the Sussex Ornithological Society; a representative of the owners of the land in the proposed extension (DL Paul & Sons Ltd) and an additional Councillor from SUDC.

Following the Local Government Act 1974 Seaford Urban District Council were disbanded and ownership of their assets, including the Seaford Head Estate, was transferred to Lewes District Council. The Constitution was amended to reflect this change of circumstances with Lewes District Council (2 members), Sussex Trust for Nature Conservation Ltd (2 members), Seaford Natural History Society (1), Sussex Ornithological Society (1) and Mr D W Paul, representing the landowners of the eastern extension.

East Sussex County Council, as owners of the Seven Sisters Country Park, were managing land which abutted the Reserve, so in 1974 it was agreed that the Ranger at the Seven Sisters Country Park (John Gascoigne) would be seconded to work as honorary warden in the Local Nature Reserve for two days a week. Whether this was all of the Reserve or just part of it is not recorded.

~ *Governance* ~

An amended constitution was agreed in 1983 which expanded the Committee to 10 delegates: Lewes District Council (3); Sussex Trust for Nature Conservation (2); Seaford Natural History Society (1); Sussex Ornithological Society (1), the tenant of Chyngton Farm, a representative from the Coastguard Cottages and Mr D W Paul.

Mr Gascoigne (who was also a member of the Seaford Natural History Society) continued to work on the Reserve for two days a week until 1985 when he retired and his place was taken by Mr Stagg. He was only in post for 12 months before Monty Larkin took over the job and Monty served (with some assistants and assistance – see Appendix 2) until 1993.

At this time, Management Committee Meetings were held four times a year; one meeting would be the AGM and one a site meeting. Monty Larkin, recalls *"many of the Committee meetings held at The Downs* [now the Leisure Centre] *were rather like social events with the amiable Ted Sales in the Chair."*

These Ranger services were provided free of charge by East Sussex County Council until 1988 when it was agreed by the Committee that 52 days per year would be purchased from the County Council at a cost of £2,000. Three years later this was raised to £2,400 plus an honorarium of 10% of any filming fees.

The following year the Committee were informed *"that the County Councils of East and West Sussex, relevant District Councils and the Countryside Commission were to establish the Sussex Downs Conservation Board (SDCB) from 01/04/1992. This would mean that the management of the Ranger service would be transferred to the new Board."* This transfer of responsibility resulted in a new Ranger, Paul Ling, taking over in 1993; and in 1994 the SDCB took over responsibility for the Sussex Downs Area of Outstanding Natural Beauty (AONB) and for managing filming rights in the Reserve.

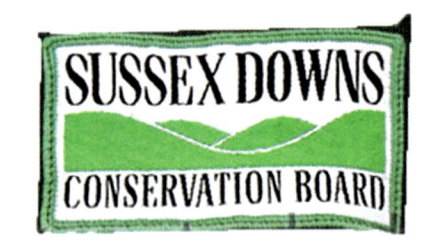

The Management Committee's Honorary Secretary (Mr T Hayward?) prepared a draft revised version of the constitution and terms of reference for consideration at the AGM in 1993. It was agreed to ask the National Trust, who had recently purchased Chyngton Farm, if they wished to be represented on the Committee. They obviously did, and the new Constitution was ratified early the following year. The Committee continued to focus on the main areas of the Reserve [see section on Land Management] but were able to liaise with this

~ *Governance* ~

new National Trust representative to ensure that there was joined-up thinking within the Reserve as a whole.

A change of personnel in 1996, with the arrival of Neil Featherstone, resulted in his suggestion that the 10% honorarium agreed in 1991 should be used to fund the training of volunteers working on the Reserve. Unsurprisingly his idea was enthusiastically approved.

The Constitution and Terms of Reference were tinkered with again in 1996, with only minor amendments to the wording and remaining at 11 members on the Committee, albeit with a slightly different representation: Lewes District Councillors (3); Sussex Wildlife Trust (2), East Sussex County Council (1), Seaford Natural History Society (1), Sussex Ornithological Society (1), National Trust (1); Chyngton Farm tenant farmer, and a representative from the Coastguard Cottages.

The formation of Seaford Town Council in 1999 and the proposed phased restoration of assets, including the part of Seaford Head which had been in the custodianship of Lewes District Council since 1974, caused another revision of the constitution with the Committee inviting the Town Council to appoint a representative. Interestingly the Chairman of the Management Committee, Dr Jill Rosser, who had been a Seaford Member of Lewes District Council, became the Town Council representative.

The Millennium brought another change of Ranger when Fran Southgate replaced Neil Featherstone; it also brought another change in the Constitution – allowing for the addition of a representative from The Society of Sussex Downsmen (now the South Downs Society) – as well as provision to appoint a Vice-chairman. Representatives now from: Seaford Town Council (1), Lewes District Council (3), Sussex Ornithological Society (1), Sussex Wildlife Trust (2), National Trust (1), Society of Sussex Downsmen (1), Seaford Natural History Society (1), East Sussex County Council (1), South Downs Conservation Board (1), Coastguard Cottages (1) and Mr D W Paul (former landowner advisor).

In 2003 it was reported that Seaford Town Council had requested permission for an additional representative to be included on the Management Committee – namely Dr Rosser who had not stood for re-election at the recent polls. This was agreed and the Constitution was amended to reflect this: Lewes District Council (3); Seaford Town Council (2); Sussex Ornithological Society (1); Sussex Wildlife

~ *Governance* ~

Trust (1); National Trust (1); Society of Sussex Downsmen (1); Seaford Natural History Society (1); East Sussex County Council (1); South Downs Conservation Board (1); Coastguard Cottages (1) and Mr DW Paul. It was further agreed that, in addition, SDCB and English Nature could have a non-voting representative.

There followed a few quiet years apart from a change of Rangers, with Fran Southgate being replaced by Simon McHugh in 2001 and Simon being replaced by Tracey Younghusband in 2005.

The announcement that the South Downs would become a National Park in April 2011 prompted a transitional management arrangement in which the South Downs Conservation Board, responsible for the Sussex Downs AONBs, was, in 2005, merged with the East Hampshire AONB and then immediately rebranded as the South Downs Joint Committee (SDJC) to oversee the formation of a National Park Authority. This Joint Committee was itself disbanded in 2012, its job done.

Meanwhile, 2005 was also the year of the third phase of devolution of assets from Lewes District Council to Seaford Town Council, with the transfer of the Seaford Head estate (Local Nature Reserve and golf course), the Crouch, the Salts recreation ground and parts of Chyngton Farm. This prompted a change to the Constitution, with a swap to 3 Town Council members and only 2 from Lewes District Council. It also meant partnership working between the South Downs Joint Committee and Seaford Town Council for oversight of the Reserve, with the Management Committee continuing to actively monitor and engage with the work being done.

The SDJC provided Ranger services in much the same way as its predecessors had done until it was disbanded following the establishment of the National Park Authority in 2011. The Management Committee were informed that the new National Park Authority would not be providing a Ranger service and that East Sussex County Council, Natural England and the Town Council had handed over responsibility for the Town Council owned part of the Reserve to the Committee. It was noted with dismay that the Committee had no funds or income to employ a Ranger, but was able to fund a Management Plan which subsequently formed the core of the Service Level Agreement devised for the management of the Reserve.

~ *Governance* ~

National Park status prompted yet another change to the Constitution with a representative from the National Park Authority, instead of the SDJC, being included on the Management Committee. This was ratified in October 2011 with the Committee membership now 16, comprised of: Lewes District Council (2); Seaford Town Council (3); Sussex Ornithological Society (1); Sussex Wildlife Trust (2); National Trust (1); Society of Sussex Downsmen (1); Seaford Natural History Society (1); East Sussex County Council (1); National Park Authority (1); Coastguard Cottages (1); Natural England (1) and Tenant Farmer (1).

This was new territory for the Town Council as well as for the Management Committee who invited the Sussex Wildlife Trust (SWT) to outline the aims and objectives of that organisation and to talk about how they could help manage the Seaford Town Council owned portion of the Reserve (see separate section on Land Management). This was favourably received and discussions about the terms of a possible Service Level Agreement took place within the Town Council. It took a while, but in February 2012 the Committee was informed that surveys and habitat maps were being produced to feed information into the new draft Management Plan. This new plan was ready for input and comments from Committee Members by November and included a schedule of works for a 6 year period and 8 key management objectives: coastal cliff; grazing; scrub work; Harry's Bush; salt marsh; access/public rights of way; awareness and monitoring.

Concern was still being expressed about a lack of Ranger services but early in 2013 a contract was awarded to Sussex Wildlife Trust and the current Ranger, Sarah Quantrill, started work on 4th June. In 2015, halfway through the contract period, progress was reviewed and it was reported that the SWT Senior Ecologist, Graeme Lyons, had visited the site and was pleased with how much had been done by Sarah and her team of local volunteers.

In 2014 the Constitution was again amended to reduce the number of Members to 15.

In June 2015 the Management Committee were told that Seaford Town Council and Sussex Wildlife Trust would be meeting to discuss the possibility of a longer term management lease for the site. The two organisations worked together to formulate a plan to lease the Reserve to the SWT on a 25 year peppercorn lease

~ Governance ~

Seaford Town Mayor, Councillor Linda Wallraven (forefront right) and Sussex Wildlife Trust Chairman, Carole Nicholson, shake on the new lease watched by Sussex Wildlife Trust Ranger, Sarah Quantrill (left of centre), and some of the local volunteers. August 2017.
- Image from STC website.

as well as guaranteeing an annual payment from the Town Council to SWT for the Ranger and the materials necessary to run the Reserve. This long-term lease would enable external funding to be sought towards conservation work and specific projects within the Reserve.

The Committee were in full support of SWT being awarded this contract, and in the summer of 2017 it was announced that a new 25 year lease had been signed.

This has already paid dividends as funding has been secured from the Heritage Lottery Fund for a two-year Seaford Community Wildlife Project launched in 2017. The SWT Project Officer, Nikki Hills, explained the scheme: *"Children at*

~ Governance ~

local Primary Schools will be able to cycle with me and my volunteers to the beach or nature reserve to enjoy Wild Beach sessions. At the beach they will learn about tides, shingle, the plants and wildlife you can find on the strandline and also about the creatures living below the waves. I will also visit schools and community groups working with people of all ages and helping them to find out about and encourage wildlife living in their patch. I will also be helping to develop 'wild areas' within school grounds."

The Management Committee previously met three or four times a year with one of those meetings being a site visit and, therefore, very hands-on. Under the new arrangements it now provides a forum to oversee the work programme designed to deliver the objectives of the Management Plan, liaise with the Ranger, and be consulted on anything which could impact on the site.

Special mention must be made of some long-serving members of the Committee (in order of years' service). This list is not exhaustive; of necessity there are many omissions for which I apologise unreservedly:

R Batchelor (Bob) joined the committee in 1971 representing the Sussex Ornithological Society until his retirement in 1981. He was the only person authorised to ring migrating birds and provided an annual report and bird count. He campaigned, unsuccessfully, for various redundant structures to be repaired and equipped as hides to observe the migrating birds.
Service to the Committee = 10 years.

D H Harvey representing The Nature Conservancy (now Natural England) was one of the four original people to form the Management Committee in 1969. He was heavily involved in preparing the first Management Plan which was finally adopted in 1980. He is not mentioned in the Minutes after 1979.
Service to the Committee = 10 years.

H J Harrison was one of the original four people to form the Management Committee in 1969. He served as Honorary Secretary from 1971 to 1977 when he relinquished the post due to ill health. He continued to serve on the Committee as the Sussex Naturalists Trust Ltd (now Sussex Wildlife Trust) representative until 1983, and died in 1986.
Service to the Committee = 14 years.

~ Governance ~

Kathleen Amoore was the Sussex Wildlife Trust representative on the Management Committee from 1982 until 1996 and was Chairman 1991 – 1996. She retired in her 90th year and died aged 96, in 2003. Upon her retirement she was presented with a photograph of the Cuckmere Cottages and cliffs in winter in grateful recognition of her service to the Committee. She had also been secretary of the Seaford Natural History Society for 23 years, also retiring from that role in 1996. Three black poplars were planted in her memory alongside the public footpath in the (then brand new) Ouse Estuary Reserve.
Service to the Committee = 14 years.

Chris Lowmass representing the Sussex Ornithological Society joined the Management Committee in 2005, becoming Chairman in 2011. In 1986 he undertook a butterfly survey on the Reserve recording 19 different species.
Service to the Committee = 14 years and counting.

Councillor E L Sales (Ted) joined the Management Committee as a Lewes District Council representative in 1977 becoming Chairman almost immediately and continued in this role until his retirement in 1991 when he was presented with a suitable token of the Committee's esteem. Unfortunately there is no record what this token of esteem was.
Service to the Committee = 14 years.

Tony Thorpe joined the Management Committee in 2000 as the representative for the Society of Sussex Downsmen, now the South Downs Society. He was Vice-chairman from 2006 until 2012.
Service to the Committee = 19 years and counting.

A W Heathcote (John) represented the Seaford Urban District Council on the Management Committee from 1971 until 1974 when the SUDC was disbanded, serving as chairman 1972 – 1974. He then took over the role of Honorary Treasurer until he retired in 1994.
Service to the Committee = 23 years.

G E C Hemingway (Chris) representing the Seaford Natural History Society, campaigned for the creation of the Local Nature Reserve and was one of the

~ *Governance* ~

original four people to form the Management Committee in 1969. He served continuously until his death in 1992.
Service to the Committee = 23 years.

Patrick McCausland joined the Management Committee as a Lewes District Council representative for Seaford in 1992. He retired from local politics in 1999 but continued to serve on the Committee, as the Sussex Wildlife Trust representative instead. He was Chairman from 2003 – 2011.
Service to the Committee = 27 years and counting.

David W Paul representing DL Paul and Sons Ltd, the owners of Chyngton Farm and the land which was added to the Reserve on the eastern side in 1975 (now owned by the National Trust); joined the Committee in 1971 and retired in 2000 when the NT appointed their own representative. He did a lot of physical management work on the Reserve in its early years cutting back grass and scrub and providing cattle for grazing.
Service to the Committee = 29 years.

Land Management

Having successfully petitioned for the land designation it must have then been quite daunting to decide how best to manage the land for the benefit of the wildlife and the public – continuing access being a major concern on *"land which is held by the Council as a public walk and pleasure ground to which the general public have unrestricted access."*

Following the official Local Nature Reserve designation in February 1969, the fledgling Management Committee held their first meeting the following August. It was agreed by the four Members (see separate section on Governance) that the Sussex Naturalists Trust Conservation Corps be told of the need for scrub control and asked if they could help; and also that Nature Conservancy should be asked to advise on the grass cutting work needed and to provide the [Seaford Urban District] Council with a Management Plan.

Enjoying the view - *Photo by Alison Baker*

But at the end of 1971 it was the Sussex Naturalists Trust (now Sussex Wildlife Trust [SWT]) who were recommending the clearance of 16 acres of scrub on land east of Hope Bottom and that the path to Hope Gap should be widened – suggesting that the area was very overgrown. The Natural History Society representative, Mr Hemingway, in his report back to the Society said *"the greatest concern was to keep the [Hope Valley] triangle free of [scrub] while in the valley it needed to be kept in check, to prevent it overgrowing the Moon Carrot."* The Management Committee agreed to ask Seaford Urban District Council to provide two men with a tractor and flail for one day to do this work and to ask the Interact Club of Seaford to clear away the cuttings.

~ Land Management ~

The Minutes of the following meeting report that *"Mr Paul [owner of Chyngton Farm] had spent 12 hours clearing scrub himself on the flat ground at the bottom of the path at Hope Gap and about 5 acres at the top to the east of the path. Two small parties of Scouts had started clearing this up but this had not been finished."* Winter management work consisted of the cutting of grass, scrub, thistle and Hogweed and the BTCV also did some work widening the path to Hope Gap.

So despite the appointment in 1974 of John Gascoigne, warden at the Seven Sisters Country Park, as the first Honorary Warden in the Reserve (with the understanding *"that a primary duty would be to prevent unauthorised shooting on the Reserve"*), management of the site throughout the 1970's was very *ad hoc* using whatever voluntary labour was available – although there was preparation work going on in the background.....

In 1974 the need for a Management Plan, originally mooted in 1969, was again back on the agenda of the Management Committee. Mr Harvey, the Nature Conservancy representative suggested *"that this be based on a five year programme, setting out objectives and works needing to be done in order to achieve those objectives in an orderly manner."* He proposed that the various areas of interest in the Reserve should be plotted on to a large scale plan with an indication as to what work or other action was required in those areas in order to preserve their present environmental interest or, where necessary, improve it. Mr Harvey undertook the initial preparation of the map and it was suggested that *"the Seaford Natural History Society should be asked to help with this"*. The only mention in the Society Minutes is a request for volunteers to help with a survey of Seaford Head – and no record from either source of whether this was actually done.

Later that same year *"Mr Harvey had marked on a plan*

Hope Bottom - *Photo by Alison Baker*

~ Land Management ~

of the Reserve his suggestions for the division of the area into sections for the purpose of preparing the Management Plan, see map below, and passed this to Mr Hemingway (SNHS representative) for his comments on the proposed divisions. It was hoped that the Natural History Society would undertake the necessary work next year".

There is no record of what Mr Hemingway's comments were, or whether the Society completed any of the work, but probably not as, after several years with no further mention of the project it was announced in 1979 that work had begun on a detailed management plan but this would *"require a considerable amount of work"* and that *"there was much evidence of neglect in parts of the Reserve which warranted an on-going programme of conservation which would stem from the Management Plan."* This 'considerable amount of work' was obviously finished pretty promptly this time because in 1980 the first Management Plan was approved and it remained in use until 2000.

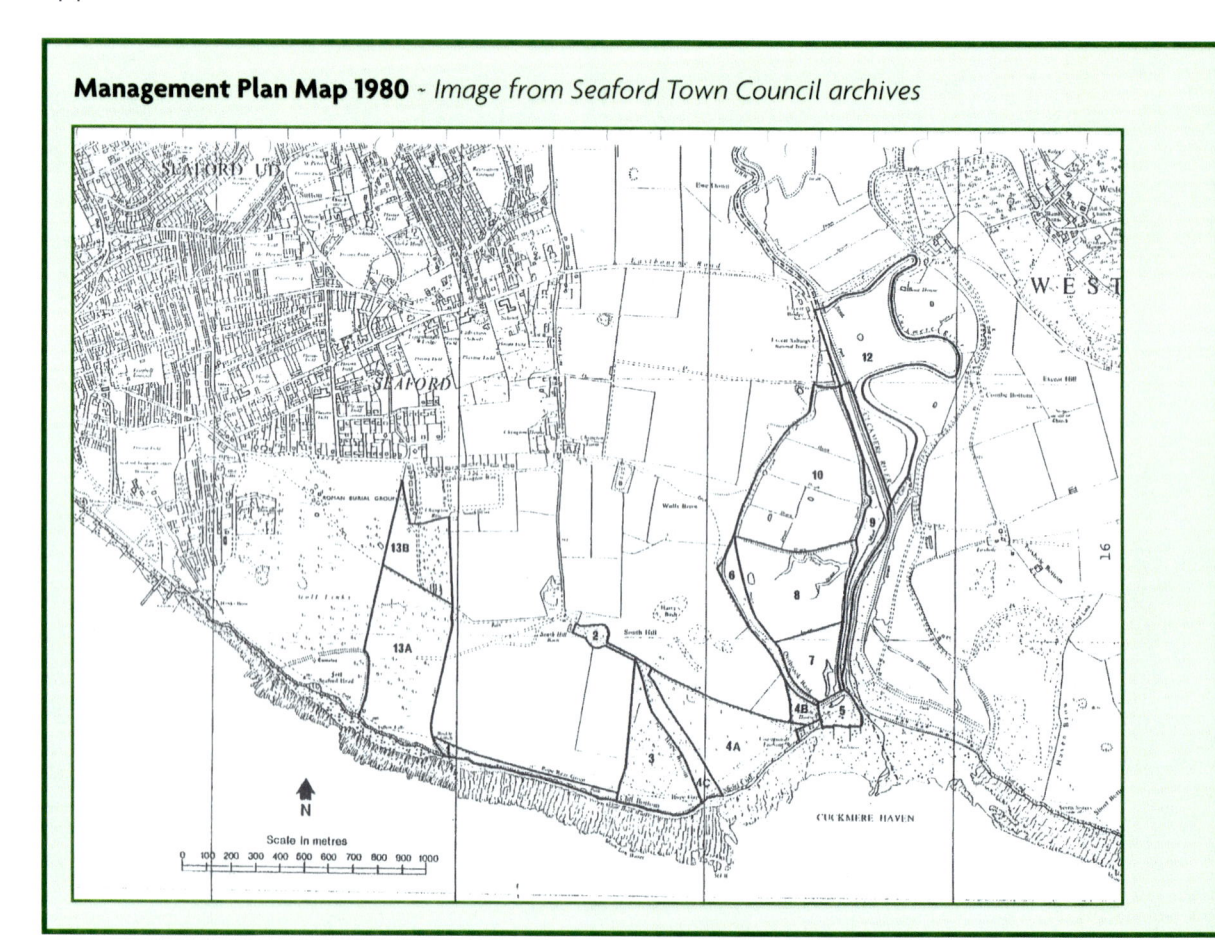

Management Plan Map 1980 - *Image from Seaford Town Council archives*

~ *Land Management* ~

N.B. Although the Management Plan covered the whole of the Local Nature Reserve, in practice only sections 2, 3, 4a, 4c, 13a and 13b received regular attention. Compartments 6, 7, 8, 9, 10 and 12 were part of Chyngton Farm and managed by its owners, DL Paul & Sons (see separate section on Governance).

Cattle were grazed annually on the *'main grass area'* [4a] from the winter of 1974, and only two years later it was noted that this had resulted in a major improvement to the native flora. Also in 1976 encroachment of scrub was noted to the west of Hope Bottom and the need to re-cut rides on the Seaford Head Estate generally, but there is no documentation of any physical work being done on the site to enhance habitats for wildlife or new paths being cut to manage the public access. This led to concern about overuse of footpaths causing deterioration and it was reported shortly afterwards that the creation of an extra footpath had relieved the pressure on the path in Hope Bottom, which had been widened.

Key to numbered sections:

13a & 13b = rear of Lullington Close to the coast adjacent to the golf course
2 = turning circle by South Hill Barn
3 = land between the farmer's fields behind South Hill barn and the path down to Hope Gap from the car park
4c = the main path down to Hope Gap from the car park at South Hill Barn
4a = land between the path down to Hope Gap and the left hand boundary with Chyngton Farmland.
4b = the land around the memorial to the Canadian soldiers, NW of the Coastguard Cottages
5 = the lagoon below the Cottages
6 = a thin strip of land between the fields and Outbrook Bank, the higher ground where the Vanguard Way goes towards the A259
7, 8 & 10 = the low-lying land between the Vanguard Way and the MHW line
9 = the tidal strip alongside the Cuckmere River
No number 11
12 = land between the new cut and the meanders (the Seaford Parish boundary is down the middle of the original meandering river course.)

~ Land Management ~

In 1982 the County Ecologist, Mr Dean, reported on the success of the management of scrub and coarse grasses by means of cattle grazing in compartment 4a. The scheme was then extended to include grazing by sheep. The area concerned extended from South Hill Barn to the Coastguard Cottages, this presumably being the 'main grass area' referred to in the 70's when cattle grazing commenced. Sheep grazing was discontinued in 1987 following the death of two sheep found at the base of the cliffs.

In 1985 Michael Stagg replaced John Gascoigne who had served 11 years as honorary warden and he, in turn, was replaced by Monty Larkin a year later. In 1988 the Management Committee began paying East Sussex County Council for their Ranger services, employing Monty, either on his own or with assistants/assistance for one day a week (see Appendix 2). He was in post for 7 years and recalls *"enjoying the variety and numbers of flowers against the back-drop of the fabulous cliff scenery."*

An artist at work painting the 'fabulous cliff scenery'
- Photo by Alison Baker

Occasionally there is a mention of the weather, usually in relation to grass cutting being late or cancelled because of excessive rain, but in early 1988 it was reported that rides in 13b would be cleared of fallen trees and bushes caused by the recent hurricane. It was later noted that the trees at Harry's Bush were virtually all sycamores and that it would be more beneficial to wildlife if replacements for those lost in the storm in 1987 included different species. Hazel, wayfaring, dog rose, field maple, holly, hawthorn and beech were chosen.

By the 1990's the Management Committee was actively managing the site to improve habitats and the visitor experience. Main pathways were cleared and scallops created by pushing back the scrub. This combined with some 'secret'

~ Land Management ~

glades were intended to provide good bird and invertebrate habitat.

Paul Ling, Ranger from 1993-1996, led a project to restore the dewpond adjacent to South Hill Barn which had been reinstated in 1988 (see separate section on the Dewpond). Footpaths were being improved, including clearance work to develop a more winding track to Hope Gap; trees were being coppiced, weeds and brambles were being tackled systematically, and grass was being cut, baled and removed twice a year.

Common Lizard - *Photo by Clare Mayers, SNHS*

In 1993 the National Trust (NT) commissioned a survey of the Chyngton estate recently purchased by them with a view to exploring the practicalities of producing a combined Management Committee/ NT management plan. Despite it being mentioned several times in the Minutes there is no record of a joint document ever being written or approved. The land which had been farmed by the Paul family was formed into an agricultural tenancy by the National Trust, and the tenant farmer became a representative on the Management Committee, thereby maintaining the opportunities for liaison in areas of joint interest.

In 1995 it was reported that English Nature had offered to meet with Members of the Management Committee to discuss the long term management of the Reserve. This was welcomed and it was noted that it would give

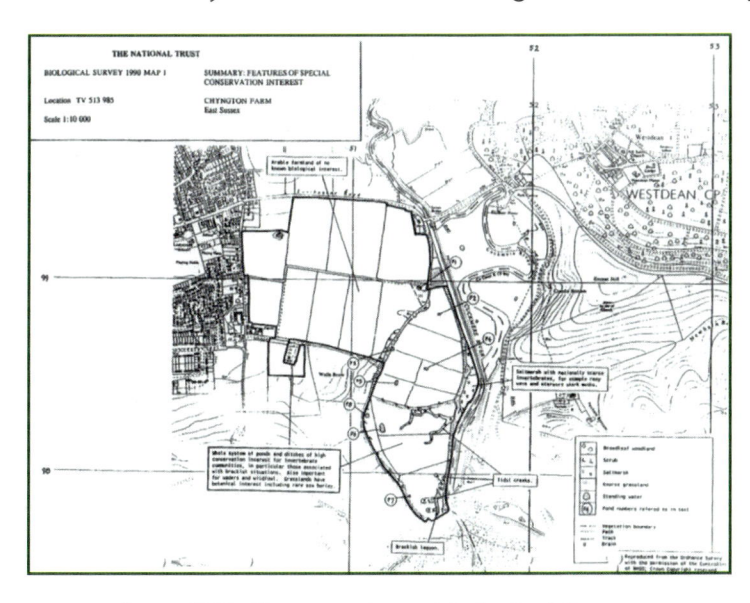

Extract from 1993 Chyngton Farm Biological Survey
~ Image from Seaford Town Council archives

~ *Land Management* ~

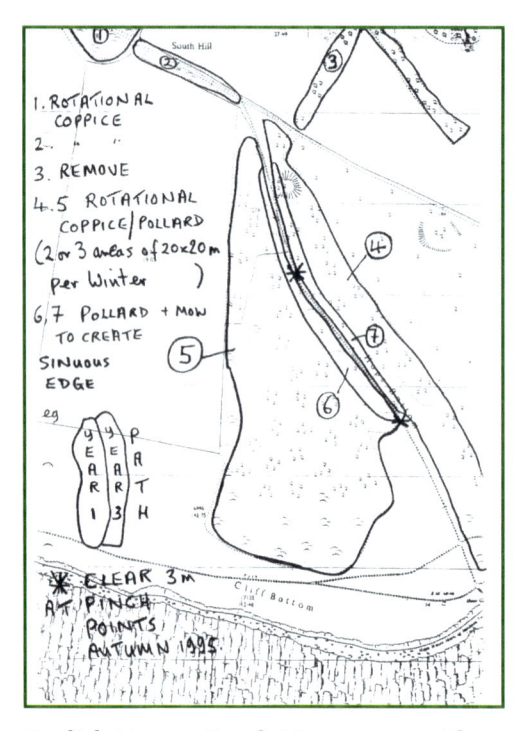

English Nature Scrub Management Plan
- Image from Seaford Town Council archives

them the opportunity to discuss clearing the islands of scrub next to the path between the road to the Coastguard Cottages and the Hope Gap steps. It was subsequently noted that *"three areas of scrub coppiced down the valley sides leading to Hope Gap had been dead hedged to prevent easy access to the public and arranged to be invisible to the normal access paths......* and *"the coppiced areas in the scrub cover towards Hope Gap will be extended [in the] autumn along with areas along the track to the Cottages."*

This was a three year project to create a varied age and structure, with the Ranger, now Neil Featherstone, informing the Management Committee in 1997 that *"the scrub management programme that was started in 1995 continued with the three areas of coppiced scrub along the sides of the track to Hope Gap being extended during the autumn period."* It was agreed that the project *"had been generally successful in achieving their aims. However proposals for 'scrub islands' had not been successful as the only regeneration in the cleared areas had been of undesirable plant species. The Ranger proposed coppicing the scrub around its edge to the depth of 1-2 metres which would produce an increased edge effect. This would, hopefully, facilitate the growth of 'desirable grassland tall herb species' and arrest the invasion of the chalk grassland by the scrub thereby increasing the use of the scrub by the resident birds."*

Path on Seaford Head - *Photo by Alison Baker*

~ Land Management ~

At a site meeting in 1998, as the three year project neared completion, *"it was agreed that the scrub management was proving to be a great success. It appeared to be an ideal technique and had not reduced the visual amenity of the area."* Ever mindful of that visual amenity, the Ranger reported that the *"regime adopted over last three years will be continued with three or four areas to be coppiced in the scrub aligning the pathway to Hope Gap. The previous areas have regenerated and provide a young scrub habitat of various ages in amongst the older surrounding scrub. The new areas will be placed out of sight as much as is practicable and in the areas of existing scrub that has not been coppiced recently."*

Wasp Spider
~ Photo by Paul Baker, SNHS

At the following meeting the Ranger *"drew attention to the two dense areas of scrub east and west of the path to Hope Gap and reported that this year he intended to scallop the edges on approximately 20% of the scrub as per his report to the last meeting. Over the next five years he hoped to introduce variation to the edges in the interests of sound ecological management. In the three areas previously coppiced the elderberry was regenerating favourably but the hawthorn and blackthorn were relatively slow. He proposed extending these areas again in [the winter of] 1998. The Ranger proposed reducing the wild privet to 2m on the south facing bank to the west of Hope Gap to allow regeneration of the turf and reduce damage by rabbits."*

Having instigated a rolling programme of works, the 'noughties' consisted of a continuation of the successful scrub works and grass mowing. Specific management to improve habitats was also now undertaken with the new Ranger, Fran Southgate, reporting that *"some 'secret' glades made by the volunteers should provide us with some wonderful bird and invertebrate habitat."*

A new draft Management Plan had been drawn up in 1998/99 and submitted to English Nature, a statutory consultee for all work proposed to be done on the Reserve, for their consideration. In 2000 the Ranger, Fran Southgate, reported that it had been approved and would now be circulated to Members. At the following meeting it was noted that *"printing problems meant that the final version had not*

~ *Land Management* ~

been distributed yet," but eventually the *"plan was considered with regard to its adoption. A few minor amendments were made and it was resolved that the plan be adopted by the Committee."*

In 2002 it was agreed with the Head Greenkeeper of the golf course that the public footpath and open area to north and northwest of Lullington Close and adjacent to the 13th fairway would not be mown until late August because *"these areas have good populations of wild flowers and associated invertebrates which may be flowering or active until late summer."* The Ranger, Simon McHugh, also reported having contacted the Head Greenkeeper regarding *"the flailing of scrub edges and the mowing of grass and flowers along rides of the parts of the golf course that overlapped with the Reserve thus reducing the cover for sheltering birds and a reduced food supply. The Head Greenkeeper had agreed to cut only one side of the ride each year, reducing the disturbance to the wildlife."*

Vestal Cuckoo Bee - *Photo by Paul Baker, SNHS*

There is no record of when the annual grazing which started in the 1970's ceased, but also in 2002 the Ranger suggested *"reinstating the grazing by livestock to reduce the amount of mowing needed and improve the area for wildlife."* Tom Masters, the tenant farmer at Chyngton Farm, was agreeable to the idea of doing this for

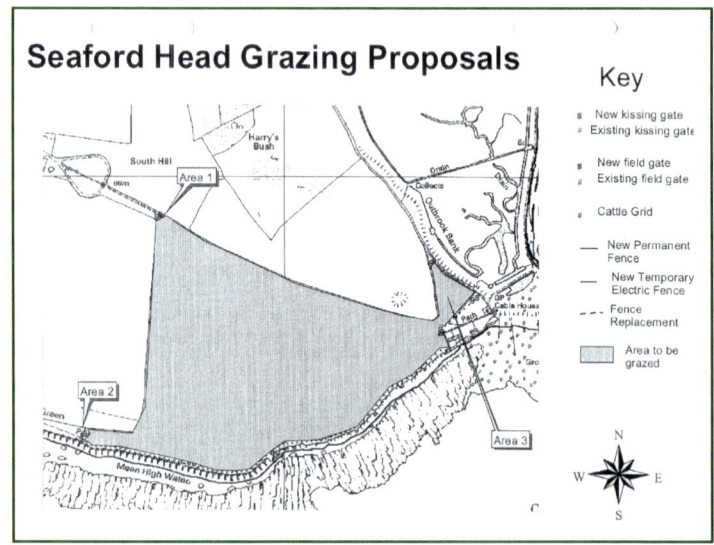

Image from Seaford Town Council Archives

36

~ Land Management ~

two months each year on *"the large open grassy area between the Coastguard Cottages and the Hope Gap steps"* and this began in August/September 2003. It was subsequently reported that there had been no adverse reactions from the public to the cattle grazing, the cattle were in good health and the experiment appeared to have been successful. The Society of Sussex Downsmen were thanked for contributing £2,000 towards the cost of fencing the scheme.

The success of this scheme was, perhaps, the catalyst for considering the possibility of grazing sheep again. The English Nature representative, Jon Curson, reiterated *"that grazing was the only way to preserve the nature of the open grassland"*, and opined that this would be particularly beneficial in an area to the south of Lullington Close and the Ranger drew up plans for fencing, gates and a water supply.

The same year it was noted that the area immediately to the east of the Hope Gap Steps was being 'squeezed' by coastal erosion and scrub encroachment which threatened the colony of scarce [Potter Flower] mining bees which were present in that area. The Ranger, still Simon McHugh, would *"cut back the scrub/privet by approx. 20 metres from the 'pinch point' to the east of the Hope Gap Steps during the winter in order to extend the foraging opportunities for the mining bees with the expectation that ground flora will include species which were of benefit to them."*

Linnet wildlife watching
- Photo by Clare Mayers, SNHS

But it wasn't always the flora and fauna which occupied the Management Committee. Following a site meeting in 2004 Members reported that *"a review of the safety measures along the cliff edge had been undertaken following the recent fatality at the Golf Course. At a site meeting the clear signage at several points along the cliff edge, the fencing where paths at right angles to the cliff edge emerged and the well mown and clearly visible path which ran at a safe distance from the cliff edge were all inspected. It was unanimously agreed that there is no need for additional cliff edge safety measures."*

By 2005 the grazing scheme was on the agenda again, concern having been expressed to the Management Committee with regard to damage to botany

~ Land Management ~

caused by the cattle who had churned up some areas of the path. The Ranger restated that the overall effect of the scheme should improve the botany of the area and Mr Curson suggested providing fewer animals for a longer period, and it was agreed that the *"removal of scrub along the path was desirable and would help maintain public support for the scheme,"* and that the Chairman, Patrick McCausland, would talk to the press about the success and benefits of the grazing regime.

Cinnabar Moth
~ Photo by Clare Mayers, SNHS

Also in 2005 the eastern part of the Reserve was entered into the Environmentally Sensitive Areas (ESA) Scheme, a 10 year agreement which provides an annual grant to help protect nationally important areas of landscape, wildlife or historical significance in return for meeting DEFRA management plan objectives. This agreement was renewed in 2015.

It wasn't always the flora and fauna which occupied the Rangers either. Simon McHugh will never forget his time working on the Reserve recalling that he *"met my 'wife-to-be' there."* At the end of 2005 Simon left and was replaced by Tracey Younghusband. During her stewardship she remembered having to oversee unexpected situations including the wreck of the Ice Prince off Portland Bill in 2008 which resulted in a substantial amount of timber being washed up all along the south coast including the beach at Cuckmere Haven; a huge barge beached in a storm but re-floated successfully at the next Spring tide, and an enormous number of Kinder egg cases washed up covered in tar.

The following year, 2006, the Committee's own 2000 Management Plan was reviewed and, mindful of current situations like the imminent transfer of ownership from Lewes District Council to Seaford Town Council and the negotiations relating to the proposed National Park it was agreed that it *"should be a living document which can be updated as circumstances change,"* and that *"some vegetation surveys should be undertaken to ascertain how it is being affected by grazing."*

~ Land Management ~

Concern was expressed in 2008 about coastal erosion, particularly the narrow strip of Reserve land to the south of the grazing pasture behind South Hill Barn. It was agreed to write to Seaford TC expressing this concern and advising that the boundary of the Reserve may have to be moved at a future date.

Alex Stephens replaced Tracey Younghusband as Ranger at the end of 2008 and was the last before the South Downs National Park was established and Ranger services ceased to be provided. His final report stated that *"scrub clearance has taken place towards Seaford Head GC. Contractors have also cut back brambles, mown meadow near the golf course and cut hedges. The slope near Lullington Close has also been cut back to reveal steps and 20-30 cattle are currently back on site until March."*

The South Downs National Park was established on 1st April 2011 and the Management Committee, mindful of the fact that they were now without Ranger services or the funds to pay for such a service, expressed extreme concern for the future of the Reserve. A 'Friends Group' was suggested and Councillor Bob Brown volunteered to lead this scheme for a three month trial period. It was subsequently reported that costs had been sought by Seaford TC for future management of the land so it was agreed that the Friends Group idea would not be pursued.

Common Blue butterfly
- Photo by Paul Baker, SNHS

After an initial period of difficult liaison with the administration of the fledgling Local Authority, the Management Committee contacted individual Town Councillors to successfully lobby for continued maintenance in the Reserve. After a rigorous competitive tendering process, the Sussex Wildlife Trust (the only ones to have their own grazing livestock previously shown to be so advantageous on the Reserve) were the successful candidates. The Town Council also provides on-going support for the part of the Reserve within the Golf Course where the Greenkeepers maintain the rides and do other work to complement the Management Plan.

A Service Level Agreement between Seaford Town Council and the Sussex

~ Land Management ~

Wildlife Trust was signed in 2013 and Sarah Quantrill was appointed Ranger to work ten and a half hours per week. In the intervening two years the SWT had investigated funding sources including a Higher Level Stewardship Grant Scheme administered by Natural England, and commissioned Graeme Lyons (SWT Senior Ecologist) and Andy Phillips (a freelance ecologist) to survey the site and produce a Management Plan. This Plan, which featured eight key management objectives (see below) and a schedule of works for a 6 year period was approved by the Management Committee and the Town Council in 2013. It was also agreed to proceed with the application for the 10 year High Level Grant Scheme and a decision from Natural England on this is still awaited.

2013 Management Plan Maps
~ Images from Seaford Town Council archives

Key objectives:
1. Coastal cliff,
2. Grazing,
3. Scrub work,
4. Harry's Bush,
5. Salt Marsh,
6. Access/Public rights of way,
7. Awareness
8. Monitoring invasive species

Figure 7. Grassland Blocks A-F (outlined in red), management boundary (outlined in dark green), potter flower bee nest site areas (marked by green arrows).

Figure 12. Eastern side of management area (outlined in dark green), with ride management and woodland edge management (orange). (Public footpaths marked in pink.)

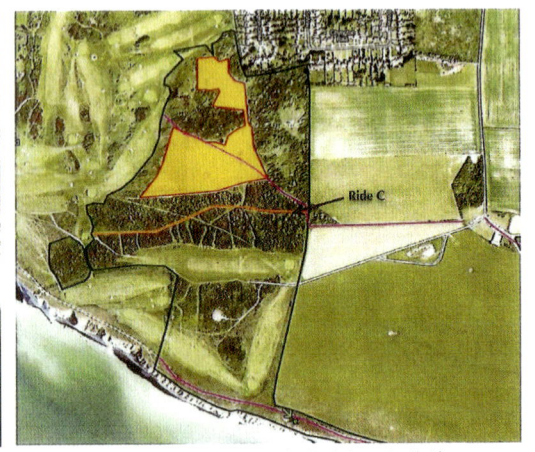

Figure 14. Western side of management area (outlined in dark green), with ride management (orange). (Public footpaths marked in pink.)

~ Land Management ~

In co-operation with Sarah Quantrill and Natural England, the National Park Authority identified funds which they could use to scallop land between Hope Bottom and Hope Gap to create a new ride which they did in the autumn of 2013. The Chairman, Chris Lowmass, subsequently reported to the Committee that *"the new ride has opened up a block of dense scrub and bramble which was not attracting any wildlife."* It was also reported that a *"volunteer group has been started to carry out work as per the Management Plan and has begun the cutting and raking of paths and scrub clearance. SDNPA Volunteers will also be helping regularly."*

Monitoring was a key component of the new Management Plan so the Committee were delighted to be informed in 2014 that the Natural History Society were about to undertake their first annual survey of Moon Carrot (see separate section on Surveys). It was noted that moon carrots are quite rare in this country; Seaford Head is one of only two known sites, so it is important to check their numbers and adjust the management plan if necessary to halt their decline. Matt Eade completed his annual Common Bird Census as he had done for many years, although sadly there are no records of these in the archives.

Autumn Ladies Tresses
- Photo by Alison Baker

The Ranger, Sarah Quantrill, reported to the Management Committee after her first year in post that as per the management plan scrub clearance had taken place; cattle grazing had been re-introduced; a suitable sheep grazing site had been identified; monitoring of the level of cliff erosion was taking place; and she had led two guided walks for the public and one for the Natural History Society during the summer. Two Japanese Knotweed plants, a very invasive species, had been identified and dealt with.

In 2015 Sarah reported that more scallops had been created on the golf course side, ride D had been widened (see top picture on previous page) and sheep grazing was going well. Path clearance had been carried out and positive

~ Land Management ~

comments received from passers-by before scrub clearance ceased for the start of the nesting season. Sarah also informed the Committee that recent shingle work had been carried out at Cuckmere Haven without any consultation and had resulted in part of the saltmarsh being destroyed (see separate section on Saline Lagoon).

A meeting to look at the habitat sites of the Anthophora retusa (Potter flower-bee) took place in May 2016 and *"it was very encouraging to show Mike Edwards, a leading bee expert in the country, the work that has been done with the volunteers. Various sightings of the bee were made and the meeting was very successful in raising awareness of the work being done by SWT and the volunteer group."*

Wood Mouse
- Photo by Clare Mayers, SNHS

At the next meeting of the Management Committee Sarah reported that the summer programme was underway and that no major scrub clearance would be undertaken until after the nesting season. Russian Vineweed and Cotoneaster, both invasive species, would be treated over the summer; cattle are grazing on the Cuckmere side of the Reserve; invertebrate surveys are to be carried out monthly, two having taken place already with help from the Natural History Society. Four guided walks for the public were planned and the South Downs National Park volunteer group had already taken part in two Big Beach Cleans at the saline lagoon and by Hope Gap Steps.

Ten sheep were grazed during the winter 2016/ 2017 on the golf course side of the Reserve and this led very quickly to a noticeable improvement on the site. Volunteer 'lookerers' kept an eye on the sheep, as they do for the cattle, particularly because two sheep had been attacked by dogs the previous year. And in the summer Sarah reported that *"works have continued in line with the management plan with the help of the volunteers. This has included re-instating the steps at the side of the golf course, giving much easier access to the Reserve and has already received positive feedback.*

"Clearance works, aided by volunteers, have continued around Hope Gap (Area E) and in the area of low bramble to the east (Area D). On the western

~ Land Management ~

side in Areas F and G low bramble and blackthorn was cleared following sheep grazing, the latter showing improvement with the presence of Common Milkwort. A new scallop was created along the eastern end of Ride C and rotational edge maintenance was started elsewhere in the Ride. SDNP volunteers focused on beach cleaning the saline lagoon; path clearance, bench maintenance and low bramble removal will continue over the summer months."

The Committee agreed to express their concern to Seaford Town Council that the proposed long-term lease for the maintenance of the Reserve by the Sussex Wildlife Trust had still not been signed off, with its financial implications for funding applications for work and projects on the Reserve. After a prolonged debate to ensure that the final details of the lease met the expectations of all parties involved in the process, it was noted with great relief in August 2017 that a new 25 year lease had been signed (see separate section on Governance).

At the October AGM of the Management Committee Sarah reported on the summer season when *"volunteers had cleared paths, picked litter, improved the ground around benches and managed grassland. Russian Vineweed regrowth had been sprayed by a contractor. Area D in the eastern area of the reserve had been extensively mown.*

"The Autumn/Winter programme has begun with clearance of cotoneaster in the west and creation of a new scallop along the Western Ride at Hope Bottom. Sheep returned to Area F on the western side in September but were removed a week later following a dog attack which left one sheep dead and another injured. A higher fence will be installed prior to the return of the sheep. Cattle-grazing is planned for Area D in the east. A Dog Awareness Day in August was supported by SDNPA Ranger, Fay Pattinson, and volunteer Marion Trew and their dogs. Guided walks during June and July were well attended, including students from Seahaven Academy."

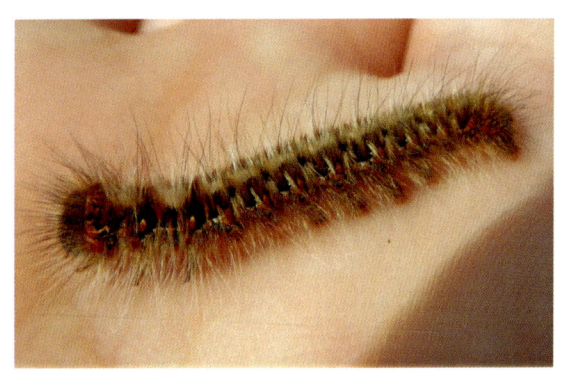

Oak Eggar Moth Caterpillar
- Photo by Clare Mayers, SNHS

The Committee were also informed that a Heritage Lottery Fund application involving the Sussex Wildlife Trust and Seaford Town Council for a Community Project Officer to undertake wildlife based projects throughout the Seaford area

~ Land Management ~

for 2 years had been approved. Nikki Hills is now in post and involved in work with local schools.

After 5 years as Ranger Sarah reflects *"I am so lucky to be the Ranger at Seaford Head Nature Reserve, it's such a fantastic site. I've seen some great wildlife and worked with lots of wonderful volunteers and I'm really proud of what we have achieved".*

> **If you would like to join the group of volunteers involved in monthly work-parties to help maintain the site you can find out more at:**
> https://sussexwildlifetrust.org.uk/get-involved/volunteer

~ Dewpond ~

Dewpond

Although we know that a pond existed adjacent to South Hill Barn when the Reserve was first established, and for many years prior to that (see below), the first mention of a dewpond in the archives was in 1975 when it was suggested that a dewpond be created. This was not pursued at the time and there is no mention of the creation or management of a dewpond in the 1980 Management Plan.

In October 1988 it was again suggested that the disused dewpond located in compartment 2 near South Hill Barn could be restored and the Ranger was asked to look into this and report back. This time there definitely was action as at the following meeting of the Management Committee in January 1989 the Ranger, Mr Cox, outlined his proposals. Sadly there is no record of what these proposals were but it was agreed that, *"this would provide a very valuable addition to the*

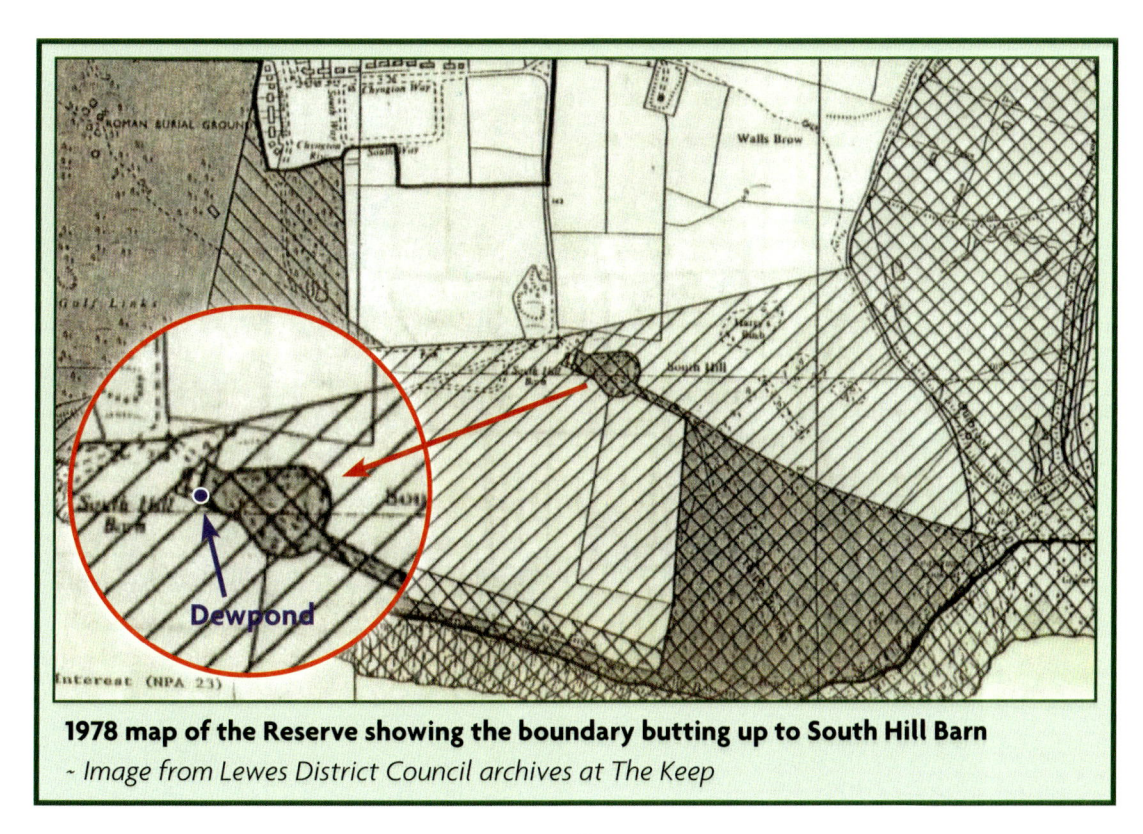

1978 map of the Reserve showing the boundary butting up to South Hill Barn
- Image from Lewes District Council archives at The Keep

~ *Dewpond* ~

Reserve but would need to be fenced and netted to keep out stray dogs. A stile would be provided so the public could view the site."

At this point it would be pertinent to digress and consider the location of this pond. The 1877 Ordnance Survey map of Seaford Head, based on a survey done in 1865 and revised in 1872, clearly shows both the dewpond and South Hill Barn. The 1978 map, shown on previous page, which was drawn up by Lewes District Council to delineate the final extension to the Local Nature Reserve, shows the boundary finishing with a broad, chunky edge adjoining South Hill Barn, consistent with the current fence-line between the Reserve and the sheep field.

Obviously the members of the Management Committee in the 1970's were the very people who had been part of the negotiation of those boundaries and they clearly believed the dewpond to be within Compartment 2 of the Reserve and this would make sense with the original mapping.

The 1980 Management Plan map has the same outline as the LDC one above, as does the land ownership map drawn up by the Sussex Downs Conservation Board in 1994. However this one, dated 2007, produced after the land had been handed back to Seaford Town Council, shows the boundary of the Reserve at South Hill Barn very differently with the Dewpond apparently no longer within the Reserve. All subsequent maps show this same profile including the latest Management Plan.

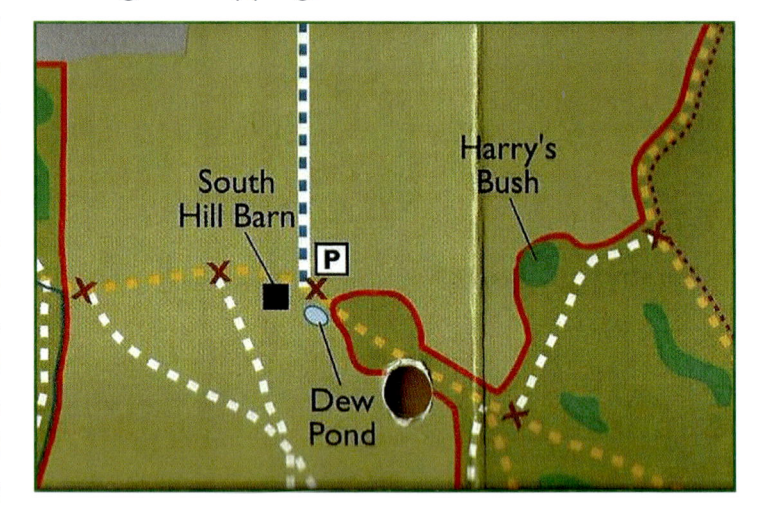

2007 Leaflet clearly showing Dewpond outside the Reserve
- Image from Seaford Town Council archives

Anyway back to our history. In June 1989 Mr Cox reported *"that the works were complete and had attracted considerable local interest. It was agreed that Mr Cox would liaise with the media to give this feature of the Nature Reserve some publicity."*

The following January 1990, the Management Committee were asked to consider a request for a memorial bench to be sited in the Reserve. In keeping with their policy of not accepting additional furniture it was agreed that they would suggest to the donor that they might like to sponsor an interpretation panel at the newly restored dewpond instead. The potential donor requested costings but the project foundered because of the length of time it took for the South Downs Conservation Board to agree an acceptable format.

The cutting of vegetation around the dewpond was listed in the winter work schedule for the Rangers in 1990, 1991 and 1992; and in June 1991 the Chairman of the Management Committee, Ted Sales, who was a Seaford representative on Lewes District Council, wrote a five-year report on the Committee's activities, noting, *"at the main entrance a dew pond has also been restored and fenced, all adding again to the diversity of interests which the Reserve provides."*

The dewpond was obviously fed from rain water guttering on South Hill Barn as concern was expressed in 1993 that the guttering was directing rain water away from the pond; and in 1994 it was noted that, *"the water level in the dewpond was not as high as expected and the Ranger was asked to check whether the drainage pipes from South Hill Barn might be defective."* At a subsequent meeting the Ranger, Paul Ling, reported that the water pipe from the barn to the dewpond had been cleared.

A site meeting attended by members of the Management Committee in August 1993 noted that three rare species had been identified in the dewpond and it was agreed that the Natural History Society be asked to identify them. It was also agreed that, *"judicious weeding in and around the dewpond should be done."* The Natural History Society agreed that there were some rare plants growing in the dewpond but, frustratingly, neither organisation named them in their records, and the Committee agreed to allow the Society to monitor these.

There are a couple of reports of the Ranger strimming vegetation around the dewpond in 1995 before it was noted during a site visit in June 1995 that *"the Pond was leaking badly and would cost about £2,000 to*

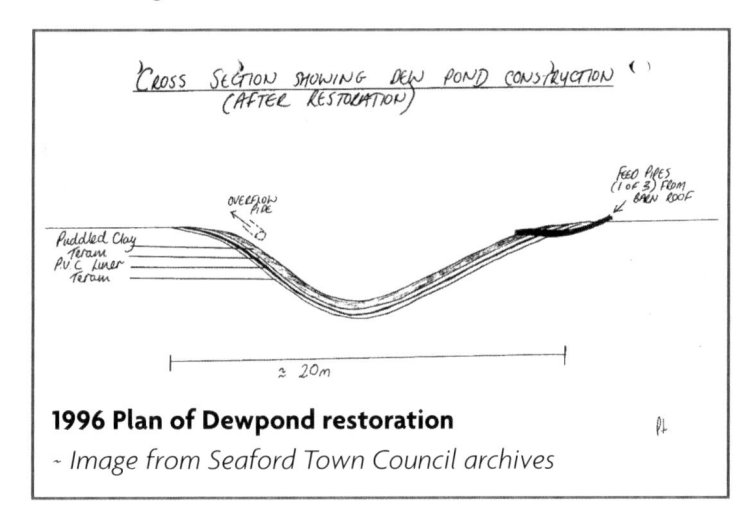

1996 Plan of Dewpond restoration
- Image from Seaford Town Council archives

~ Dewpond ~

reline." It was obviously felt that this feature was important enough to warrant the expenditure because in January 1996, the Ranger, Mr Ling, gave a presentation on the Dewpond Project (see plan on the previous page). It was agreed that the proposals for the relining of the Dewpond should be implemented.

By June it was reported that, *"the dewpond is establishing very well with all the important plants reappearing along with a wealth of insect and animal life (including large amounts of tadpoles)."*

This was obviously a popular addition to the Reserve, at least with some people. The Ranger, Neil Featherstone, reported in August 1998 that a member of the public was insisting on planting water lilies in the pond despite having been asked not to, and that frog spawn was being removed.

But invasive species were now present and the Ranger reported that *"the pond at South Hill Barn has been cleared of around 70% of the Parrots Feather that had begun to form a blanket."* This seems to be the beginning of the end for the dewpond. In November 1999 it was reported that volunteers had, *"helped clear invasive weeds which hopefully would help the rarer plants and invertebrates to flourish. A new stile and an official notice erected requesting people to neither remove nor add plant species to the pond as it may harm its conservation value".* But by February the following year the Ranger reported that, *"the dewpond was currently host to Parrots Feather*

Dewpond 2017
- Photos by Alison Baker

~ *Dewpond* ~

[and suggested] this invasive plant be exterminated before it overwhelmed some of the rarer plant specimens." This was agreed but may not have been very successful as by November the dewpond had been sprayed to kill the Crassula, (using a product approved by the Environment Agency and English Nature), with more Parrots Feather and Crassula infestations being tackled in February 2001.

A new chestnut post and rail fence was erected around the dewpond in 2002, a quote for £865 having been accepted. The Ranger, Simon McHugh, noted that the cost of this work would be included in a grant application to English Nature – and more Parrots Feather had been removed from the pond.

The dewpond appears in a Management Plan for the first time in the Plan adopted in 2003, stating *"the Dew Pond [sic] adjacent to South Hill Barn is important both historically and ecologically. It was restored in the mid-1990's as a cultural remnant of historical farming methods and is the only water 'feature' on the main part of the Reserve. It has since flourished, containing uncommon species such as Spikes Rush, Ramshorn snail, newts etc. Unfortunately the pond is also host to many invasive species i.e. Parrots Feather and Crassula which tend to be introduced by members of the public or transported on the feet/beaks of birds."*

In the Autumn of 2004 volunteers cleared the dewpond of unnamed invasive vegetation but in 2006 it was reported that, *"the pond is full of New Zealand Stonecrop (Crassula), which is a very invasive species. The most effective way of dealing with it is to deprive it of light so this will be tried."* The final mention in the Minutes is a report by Stephanie Diment, a trainee Ranger, who had tackled the Dewpond along with 8 volunteers in the summer of 2010 and cleared a large amount of the invasive weeds Australian/New Zealand Stone Crop, Parrots Feather and Canadian Pond Weed.

It is not in the part of the Reserve managed by the Sussex Wildlife Trust so it is not mentioned in their 2013 or 2017 Management Plans. Despite the confusion over the status of the dewpond as shown on maps past and present, the evidence points to the conclusion that the dewpond has always been within the Reserve; it is just no longer part of the area which is maintained and, as you can see from the photographs on the facing page, is currently somewhat neglected and unloved.

Dog Fouling

Another recurrent theme and cause for concern to the Management Committee, given the popularity and public access to the Reserve for all leisure activities, was dog fouling. In response to complaints in 1994 the Ranger, Paul Ling, *"suggested that a small area of grass adjacent to the car park at South Hill Barn should be mown to create an area where dog fouling could take place."* It was agreed that this should be trialled and the following year it was reported that *"some areas of rough grass within the circle of concrete path adjacent to South Hill Barn had been cleared but dog fouling remained a problem."* Mr Ling suggested that mown grass areas be designated dog fouling areas and it was agreed to try this.

There is no further mention in the Minutes until 1998 when the Ranger, now Neil Featherstone, *"reported that dog fouling had increased since the dog ban on Seaford seafront and suggested an awareness campaign in the local press."*

Presumably this was not effective because in 1999 the Management Committee requested permission from Lewes District Council to provide two dog waste bins *"in the car park area adjacent to the Reserve."* Later the same year the Ranger reported that the new dog bins were being well used but *"presented a draft press release relating to the problems associated with dog fouling."*

Dog Fouling reminder
- Photo by Alison Baker

This subject was back on the agenda in 2003 when it was noted that the dog bins were emptied each week by the District Council. This led to a discussion about the cost of this service and who might be asked to contribute towards it. It was agreed to draft a press release highlighting the continual problem. At the next meeting it was reported that *"a complaint had been received about dog fouling and a call for a ban on*

~ Dog Fouling ~

dogs on the Reserve. It was agreed that this would cause considerable bad feeling and would be impossible to enforce."

In 2006 the Management Committee were told that the Seaford Town Council Maintenance Supervisor would be liaising with the Ranger, Tracey Younghusband, regarding the installation of dog fouling signs, but there is no mention of how many and where they were sited, if indeed they ever were. In 2012 the Committee were discussing the subject yet again and agreed that *"more dog bins was not the answer, more signs were needed. It was noted that this is a community issue supported by the Police and Dog Warden"* and that *"Councillor White had been on the radio and spoken to the press about dog fouling, but the community had not responded. The Committee agreed it should continue to try to reduce dog fouling."*

'Awareness mornings' for dog owners have been held by Sarah Quantrill, the current Ranger, to encourage responsible dog ownership but no doubt this topic will continue to find its way on to the Agenda just as regularly in the future.

Ironically, in 2016, the Management Committee received a complaint about cow dung on the Reserve following the winter conservation grazing scheme!

Harry's Bush

Anecdotal evidence passed down over the years by owners and tenants of Chyngton Farm suggests that Harry's Bush was planted in the late 1700's as a 'picnic wood'. These were very popular at the time; somewhere to go for the day, an outing for which people were prepared to travel great distances. It would have been a project requiring great foresight as it would clearly be many years before the trees would have grown sufficiently to fulfil their purpose, and the name may well have been coined in a derisive fashion by local people who failed to see the potential of a few twigs in the ground.

Harry's Bush
- *Photo by Alison Baker*

The trees duly grew into the impressive copse we see today and at an October 1988 meeting of the Management Committee it was suggested that Harry's Bush would be a useful extension to the Reserve and it was agreed to hold a site meeting to consider the idea. This had obviously taken place by January 1989 when it was reported: *"it had been agreed that, although it was bounded by agricultural land and wouldn't be generally available to the public, Harry's Bush would be an important and valuable addition to the Reserve because: the whole area provides a useful nesting and roosting site for a number of bird species; it would facilitate management to enhance its nature conservation interest with recent fencing encouraging the growth of a valuable herb and shrub layer; the woodland habitat is not present in the rest of the Reserve, thereby adding diversity and interest; and the grazed pasture habitat type is not represented in the rest of the Reserve and will be a useful addition."*

~ Harry's Bush ~

Lewes District Council, who owned the Reserve between 1974 and 1999, obviously agreed because in January 1990 it was *"noted that the District Council had declared land adjoining the Reserve and incorporating Harry's Bush to be managed as a Nature Reserve on 29th September 1989."*

At the same meeting it was reported *"that the trees at Harry's Bush are virtually all sycamores and it was agreed that it would be more beneficial to wildlife if replacements for those lost in the storm in 1987 were replaced with a different species."* A number of nest boxes would also be provided.

Harry's Bush
- Photo by Alison Baker

In June 1990 the Ranger, Monty Larkin, reported that seven nesting boxes had been sited among the trees in Harry's Bush and it was agreed that a tree replanting scheme comprising hazel, wayfaring, dog rose, field maple, holly, hawthorn and beech should take place during 1990/91 at a cost of £196.75. The Ranger was asked to make an application for a storm re-planting grant towards the cost. This is not mentioned again so we have no idea whether it was successful or not.

Although it had been agreed at the site meeting back in 1988 that there wouldn't generally be public access, a licenced footpath and two stiles were installed east of Harry's Bush in the winter of 1994. This obviously proved popular because in 1998 the farmer requested signs for the footpath over the fields, from the track from South Hill Barn down by Harry's Bush to the footpath from the Golden Galleon (now the Cuckmere Inn) to the Coastguard Cottages *"to ensure members of the public keep to the correct line."*

Currently this area, owned by Seaford Town Council, is not part of the Reserve which is managed by the Sussex Wildlife Trust and, although on access land, is securely fenced off.

~ Hope Gap Steps ~

Hope Gap Steps

Management of a Local Nature Reserve doesn't just involve the flora and fauna, particularly at Seaford Head where public access and enjoyment has always been such a priority. Continued public access to the beach at Hope Gap is an ongoing concern and is first mentioned in the Minutes in 1979 when it was noted that *"Tenders to improve the access steps were far in excess of Lewes District Council's budget and would be reconsidered by the Amenities Committee"*.

The Amenities Committee were obviously persuaded that these were essential works as it was later reported that they had budgeted £42,000 for the work, with an additional £5,000 to be contributed from East Sussex County Council. The work was due to start in June 1979 and the Management Committee were then in negotiations with the contractor about how he would access the site to minimise damage and disturbance to the flora and fauna.

N.B. It was agreed that the contractor would also be asked to demolish the disused cable hut while he was on site but since it is still there either they changed their minds or he refused.

The official opening of the newly constructed steps at Hope Gap, by the Chairman of Lewes District Council, Councillor Miss Renee Oeters, (a former Member of the Seaford UDC) took place on 25th April 1980 with the

Hope Gap Steps
~ Photo by Alison Baker

~ Hope Gap Steps ~

Management Committee hoping that *"the public would be mindful of the fact that they are located within a Reserve"*.

Despite the enormous amount of money spent on constructing these steps it wasn't long before cliff erosion on the east side of the steps prompted the Management Committee in 1988 to request an extension to the handrail at the top of the steps. The Senior Engineering Assistant at Lewes District Council responded by stating that this extension was not needed.

By 1993 increased visitor numbers prompted the Management Committee to consider additional fencing *"to keep people away from the edge of the cliff at Hope Gap steps"*. Concern was also expressed at the condition and position of some of the signs and the memorial and it was agreed that Lewes District Council be requested to relocate the memorial stone and plaque to a more appropriate position – what memorial and plaque? The Praise Plaque erected by the English Sisters of Mary [see One-offs section]? Frustratingly there is no more information in the archives.

The Lewes District Council response is not reported but presumably not favourable, since it was agreed later the same year that the Committee *"would provide the funding for the removal and relocation of the memorial stone and plaque."* It was also agreed that the Ranger, Monty Larkin, should remove the sign and the fence to the east of the top of Hope Gap steps. It was reported at the next meeting that *"Lewes District Council be requested to use good quality board which should be attached to the fence adjoining the access gate to the steps"* but no record of the purpose of this sign.

At the same meeting it was reported that a local resident had requested permission to provide a seat in memory of his wife on the eastern side of the Reserve adjacent to the top of Hope Gap steps. Since it had been Management Committee policy since 1989 not to accept any more memorial seats it was suggested that he might like to sponsor a suitably inscribed interpretation board for the site instead. He probably didn't, since in 1996 the Ranger, Neil Featherstone,

Beach exit warning sign
- Photo by Alison Baker

~ Hope Gap Steps ~

reported that *"a member of the public wished to purchase a site interpretation board in memory of her husband."* This offer was accepted and was *"to be fixed to the fence adjacent to Hope Gap steps."*

Concerns about visitors being cut off by the tide were ever present and in 1994 the Ranger, was authorised to liaise with Lewes District Council to provide signs at the bottom of Hope Gap steps to warn visitors of the restricted exit from the beach and that these signs should say 'Last exit from Beach, no exit at Seaford'.

In 1997 the Management Committee considered a risk assessment compiled by Lewes District Council of all the coastal areas owned by them. The Report proposed providing signage consistent with that used in other Heritage Coast areas warning of the dangers of the cliff edge at key points. It was further proposed to erect additional fencing at the Hope Gap steps (across the short lengths of cliff edge which were unprotected on either side of the Steps, inside the existing fencing), at the stile leading to the cliffs from South Hill Barn and at the end of the track on the edge of the golf course. After much discussion it was agreed to approve all these recommendations.

In Millennium year the Ranger, Fran Southgate, contacted Lewes District Council regarding the undermining of the steps at Hope Gap and informed the Management Committee that the District Council proposed to introduce a more secure area of sea defences surrounding the steps. The following year it was reported that the Council had been looking at various options for the repair and reconstruction of the steps and would be consulting the Committee when the consultants had finished their scoping work. By the end of the year the Report was in. A number of different options were contained within the document which prompted a long discussion, with different Members preferring different options. Eventually it was

Hope Gap Steps
- Photo by Alison Baker

~ Hope Gap Steps ~

agreed to recommend adoption of the option *"which would allow natural processes to erode the gabion baskets structure and the cliff face. The gabions, steps and risers would progressively be made safe and the process would be carried out in two stages over a period of approximately 5 years"*. It was further agreed to stress to Lewes District Council how important it was that access to the shore at Hope Gap should be maintained.

Foreshore at Hope Gap
- Photo by Alison Baker

Lewes District Council undertook a User Survey in the South Hill Barn car park in 2003 and the Committee were invited to comment on the results. It was agreed that one of their many responses to this document would be to reiterate their view that Hope Gap Steps be retained for safety reasons.

In 2004 the recent erosion behind the steps at Hope Gap was noted and the Management Committee agreed that when informing Lewes District Council they would also express their opinion that the gabions will not last the 20 years originally expected. Two years later more concern was being expressed about continuing erosion around the steps and the importance that they should be retained. The Seaford Head estate had just been transferred to Seaford Town Council as part of the phased restoration of assets and it was agreed to bring this issue to their attention, as well as enquire as to the views of the South Downs Joint Committee (who had overview of the site during the transition from the Sussex Downs Conservation Board to the South Downs National Park Authority – see separate section on Governance).

Early the following year it was reported that the Town Clerk, Len Fisher, was arranging for a survey of the Hope Gap steps and that the South Downs Joint Committee would prefer the existing steps to be replaced with ones similar to those at Birling Gap. Concern was expressed about the condition of the fence and the lifebelt housing which had come adrift and it was agreed that the Town Council's maintenance person would undertake repairs. It was also agreed to display tide tables in the interests of visitor safety.

At the end of 2008 the Committee were informed that Seaford Town

~ Hope Gap Steps ~

Council and Lewes District Council had initiated a condition survey of the steps the previous year and their report was awaited; but it was 2009 before it was mentioned again when it was noted that the steps are free-standing and not dependent on the cliff for support. The Town Council were now waiting for an estimate from an engineer to re-profile the bottom few steps and repaint the lower section of the handrail.

Concern about the number of people getting trapped trying to get from the Hope Gap steps to the Cuckmere was again under discussion in 2009 and it was pointed out that the sign says access is not possible at high tide but actually an incoming tide is the problem. It was agreed the District Solicitor to be asked to suggest suitable wording for a new sign for Hope Gap and Splash Point.

In 2010 it was reported that there had been a cliff fall and a section of the path between the Coastguard Cottages and Hope Gap Steps was now less than two metres from the edge. It was agreed that signs were required to mark the diversion and that this should be referred to the East Sussex County Council Rights of Way Officer for guidance and to liaise with Seaford Town Council. No further mention is made of this; the next and final reference to the steps is a report in 2012 that, yet again, the steps need maintenance.

~ *Promotion and Publicity* ~

Promotion and Publicity

As early as 1974 ways of promoting the Reserve were being discussed. A nature trail was suggested but not considered feasible so it was decided to produce a leaflet guide. Mr Chris Hemingway, a petitioner for the Reserve and founder member of the Management Committee, volunteered to produce a first draft. After a satisfactory text and layout had been approved 1,000 copies in green text on cream laid paper were printed in 1977. These were made available to local information centres, schools and other *"local bodies which have an interest in natural history"*.

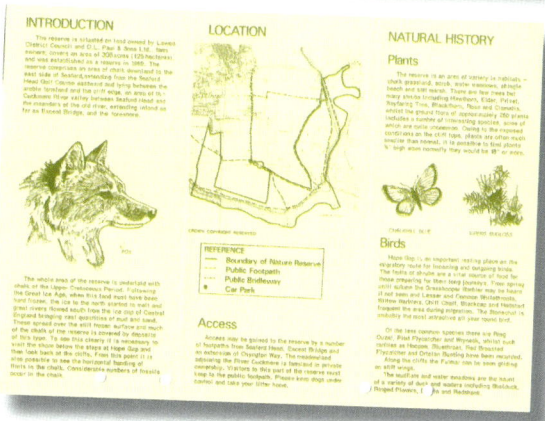

A year later stocks were exhausted and a reprint was being discussed. The western extension to the Reserve had just been confirmed so this entailed a revised map and the addition of text about the foreshore. Less than a year later, in 1980, it was once again reported that there were no leaflets left and a reprint was approved. This time it was only six months before all copies had gone and it was agreed that a further 2,000 would be printed.

In 1995 the South Downs Conservation Board requested permission to introduce a small charge for the leaflets available at the Seven Sisters Visitor Centre in an effort to restrict their removal. The Management Committee refused this request since the leaflet was freely available at the Lewes and Seaford Tourist Information

1978 Leaflet
- from SHLNRMC archives

~ Promotion and Publicity ~

1987 Leaflet
- from SHLNRMC archives

Centres. It was later reported that the leaflets had been reprinted by Lewes District Council at a cost of £55.50 for 600, just over 9p each.

There was obviously a change of heart as another reprint was commissioned in the Millennium year with the directive that they should be sold to the Tourist Information Centres in Lewes, Seaford and Eastbourne for 12p each and to the public for 20p. Honesty boxes would be placed at the Seven Sisters Country Park, Golden Galleon Public House; Seaford Library and Museum and Beachy Head Visitor Centre.

In 2006 a sub-committee was formed to update the leaflet and it was noted that the artwork of the current leaflet was still available for use. The draft copy was approved, printed, and had all gone by 2009 when 10,000 more were ordered at a cost of £840.

New leaflets were once again on the agenda in 2012 when it was agreed that they must have an attractive design to encourage people to visit the Reserve; and the following year the Committee discussed a suggestion that East Sussex County Council and the National Trust be asked to contribute towards the cost.

As well as paper leaflets, website technology had arrived, albeit somewhat reluctantly as in 2006 it was Minuted that *'a website should be considered'*. In 2008 it was noted that 'the website' (actually a link from the Town Council site) currently only consisted of a brochure and it was suggested that proper photographs and details of the wildlife commonly found on the Reserve should be added. Whether this was done or not is not mentioned but it was brought to the Committee's attention in 2011 and again in 2012 that the website needed updating.

~ Promotion and Publicity ~

In his Management Plan 2013-2017, Graeme Lyons Senior Ecologist of the Sussex Wildlife Trust noted that online representation is mainly by the Management Committee's own page on the Town Council website and that *"there is great potential for creating an enhanced and regularly updated online presence for the Reserve in partnership with the surrounding areas within the South Downs National Park. This type of community wildlife website has proved very successful elsewhere in Sussex enhancing awareness and improving community engagement".*

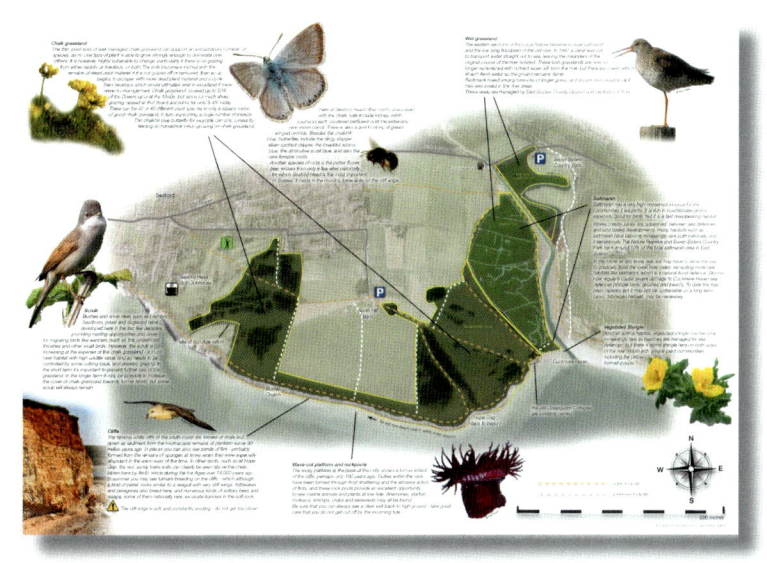

Inside of the current Leaflet
- Image from the Seaford Town Council website

In 2015 more technology was discussed by the Committee Members when it was confirmed that the proposed ILoveSeaford app would be able to include the Nature Reserve. This app has yet to be launched.

Currently the Reserve is featured on the Seaford Town Council website which gives some background information about the site and its management as well as a downloadable Nature Reserve leaflet:
www.seafordtowncouncil.gov.uk/Seaford-Head-Nature-Reserve.aspx

The Town Council also has a Facebook page:
www.facebook.com/pages/Seaford-Head-Nature-Reserve/163720333641609

and the Reserve has its own section on the Sussex Wildlife Trust website: https://sussexwildlifetrust.org.uk/visit/seaford-head which gives information about the natural history of the site as well as providing a link to the Viewranger app, which offers a range of self-guided walks, including Seaford Head, which can be accessed via a free mobile phone app.

~ *Promotion and Publicity* ~

Interpretation Boards

Interpretation Boards are not mentioned in the records until 1990 when the Countryside Management Committee requested permission to site a Geological Interpretation Panel as *"part of a programme to inform the general public about the geological features of the heritage coast area".* The request was agreed in principle but it was noted that the panel was difficult to read. It was also agreed that some of the information should be added to the Management Committee's own guide leaflet.

It had been agreed the previous year that no more requests to site memorial seats in the Reserve could be accepted. There were already so many that the wild, unspoilt nature of the Reserve was in danger of being compromised. Shortly after the discussion about the Geological Interpretation Panel another request for a memorial seat was received and it was decided to suggest to the potential donor that they sponsor an interpretation panel at the newly restored Dewpond instead.

The potential donor was obviously amenable to the idea of sponsoring a panel instead of a memorial seat for his late wife and requested costings. It was agreed that all Interpretation Boards in the Reserve should be of a standard design and the Ranger, Mr Cox, was asked to liaise with the Sussex Downs Conservation Board and report back to the next meeting.

The next mention of this project wasn't until 1994 when it was reported that the Information Officer of the Sussex Downs Conservation Board had agreed to organise a suitable design as part of the Board's Interpretive Strategy. The wheels of bureaucracy were obviously moving far too

Hope Gap Interpretation Board
- Photo by Alison Baker, 2018

~ Promotion and Publicity ~

slowly for the original enquirer as it was also reported at this meeting that he might wish to provide a kissing gate as an alternative to an interpretation board.

By 1995 Interpretation Boards had obviously been sited since the Ranger, Paul Ling, was being asked to annotate the Boards to orientate visitors to the Reserve, the Seven Sisters Country Park and Chyngton. The Ranger was also asked to prepare a report on alternative locations for the Board at the top of the Hope Gap Steps.

Buckle Church Interpretation Board
- Photo by Alison Baker, 2018

The Ranger, Neil Featherstone, reported in 1996 that a member of the public wished to purchase a site Interpretation Board in memory of her late husband. It was agreed to accept the offer, this Board to be fixed to the fence adjacent to Hope Gap steps. Later the same year he reported that this had been done.

1997 saw a rethink about the information being provided and the best way to make it accessible. It was proposed that an Interpretation Board should be sited at the Chyngton Way access point with information relevant to that area of the Reserve; another one sited at Buckle Church with information relating to the history and ecology at that point; and a third board sited at the Golden Galleon entrance with information about the river valley and the National Trust. This was agreed and it was reported later in the year that research was being carried out in respect of the 'themes' for each board. It was noted that the Board at South Hill Barn would provide orientation, information about the management of the site and some do's and don'ts. It was further noted that the Board at the Golden Galleon entrance would be paid for by the National Trust but it was unclear how the others would be financed.

By 1998 this project was well under way with the Ranger, Neil Featherstone, having presented draft panel designs, revised them in response to comments from Committee Members, circulated a second draft and had Committee approval for a final version. Sponsorship was still being sought for the estimated £3,600 cost. In 1999 the new Boards were put in position but there is no record of how they were funded.

~ Promotion and Publicity ~

It seems that the new Boards were erected but old ones not removed as only a year later the Ranger reported that he had removed an old Interpretation Board from alongside the footpath on the Golden Galleon side of the Cuckmere River.

The weather takes its toll on Interpretation Boards, particularly sunlight, so this item was back on the agenda again in 2002 when it was proposed that five Interpretation Boards should be provided, one at each of the main access points to the Reserve. The Ranger, Simon McHugh, was asked to apply to English Nature for a grant to cover the cost. The Management Committee were in agreement that all signs should be standardised and, following a discussion with the South Downs Conservation Board, who noted that there were already a number of existing signs and that adding more could have a negative impact, it was agreed that all existing signs would be removed and replaced by the five new Welcome and Interpretation Boards, the Ranger to present some draft wording and design at the next meeting in April.

South Hill Barn Interpretation Board
- *Photo by Alison Baker, 2018*

This would have been April 2004 but actually didn't appear in the Minutes again until 2006 when Committee Members were asked to look at the existing Interpretation Boards and pass their thoughts on to the Ranger, Tracey Younghusband. Again nothing seemed to happen, presumably due to funding issues, because in 2009 it was reported that the Interpretation Boards were now looking old and some were illegible. The Ranger, Alex Stephens, had obtained quotes for new ones in both oak and stainless steel and it was agreed to accept a quotation for four wooden Boards, the final draft for all four of the boards would be available for the next meeting. At the next meeting, which was spring 2010, the final proof was circulated and the Ranger was asked to contact Lewes District Council for advice following comments made by Committee Members about font, text size and colour. Again there is no written record of these panels actually being commissioned or erected but Tony Thorpe, Management Committee Member since 2000, and vice-Chairman at the time, recalls that four new oak panels were erected in 2010 and are still in use.

~ Promotion and Publicity ~

Open Days

To celebrate the Millennium, the Ranger, Fran Southgate, circulated a list of ideas for an Open Day in the summer and was congratulated for her initiative. This was felt to be an excellent idea and it was agreed that Management Committee Members *"would be invited to volunteer assistance on the day."* The event was held on the 2nd August 2000 and various activities, sadly not itemised, took place as well as a *"guided historical narrated walk."*

The Natural History Society also became involved in the event, agreeing to participate and *"to provide our display boards."* Two members were on duty at their display and *"told people about our Society."*

The Open Day was so successful that another one was held in July the following year when the Committee were informed that an *"estimated 70-100 adults and 200 schoolchildren attended."* Later the Natural History Society reported that *"seven very wet members braved the elements and 'manned' our stall, not many adult visitors were about but the school children were enjoying all of the activities organised."*

~ Rabbits ~

Rabbits

Damage caused by rabbits was first Minuted by the Management Committee in 1975 when it was agreed that Lewes District Council (LDC) be asked to authorise their control with ferrets and nets. This approach clearly failed to have the desired effect as two years later the Committee noted a considerable increase in the number of rabbits and it was resolved to ask LDC to do something about it.

Nothing more is noted until 1986 when, following a site visit by the Management Committee, it was agreed to arrange for the culling of rabbits during the winter. Concern was again expressed in 1988 about rabbit numbers on the Reserve, particularly in compartment 4a, land between the path down to Hope Gap and the northern boundary with Chyngton farmland. It was agreed to request that Lewes DC issue a licence to Peter Sole of Chyngton Lane to enable him to use ferrets and nets to reduce the population. Mr Sole was requested to keep a record of the number culled and he subsequently reported that 291 rabbits had been taken by means of long nets and ferrets between August 1988 and January 1989.

In 1989 the Management Committee discussed the subject again and it was noted that the rabbits were doing a lot of damage in compartment 4a, and agreed that the Ranger, Mr Cox, be asked to look into possible solutions. The following year it was resolved to ask the County Ecologist to identify the areas of undergrowth that could be coppiced to aid with the control of rabbits.

Rabbits were again on the agenda for the 1991 AGM when the Committee were told that 582 rabbits had been culled on the Reserve between Sept 1989 and August 1990. These numbers prompted an agreement that *"as an experiment a small area of clear turn on the western boundary of compartment 3 be wired off and rabbits excluded, with the intention of preventing further damage and giving the grass a chance to recover; also as an experiment a small area of scrub close by be cleared and wired off and the rabbits excluded to test the practicality of treating an area of scrub in a similar way."* Mr Sole continued

Rabbit eating Mooncarrot
- Image from Google.co.uk (with a bit of artistic licence by the author.)

~ Rabbits ~

to be granted an annual licence to cull rabbits on the Reserve by Lewes District Council until at least 1995 when there is no further mention of this in the archives.

In 1997 the Ranger, Neil Featherstone, suggested cutting back the scrub to the north west of Hope Gap to reduce cover for rabbits and to allow the regeneration of desirable chalk sward. The Committee noted that the proposal would reduce the cover for the rabbits and it was agreed that the Ranger should produce a written report on his coppicing proposals. His proposal was to reduce the wild privet to 2m high on the south-facing bank to the west of Hope Gap to allow regeneration of the turf and reduce damage by rabbits. This was approved but how successful this was is not recorded.

In 1999 the Ranger reported that *"the main area of wild privet will be reduced in section to the west of Hope Gap and a follow-up application of selective herbicide will prevent the regrowth and so encourage the recolonisation of more desirable grassland species and reduce the cover for the ever burgeoning rabbit population. He noted that many rabbits died of myxomatosis at the end of last year and this had had a marked effect on numbers."*

No further mention is made of rabbits or their activities until 2006 when there was a Management Committee discussion about whether it was burrowing rabbits that were taking off the top soil, particularly at Buckle Church or whether it was the wind. By 2008, although having always recognised the benefits of rabbit grazing in keeping the main grass paths closely cropped, thus also benefitting some chalk grassland plants and associated insects, the Committee were once again concerned about the rabbit numbers and the Ranger, Tracey Younghusband, was requested to seek advice from Natural England. There is no record as to whether a response was forthcoming but in March 2009, in the final mention of the archives, Mr Garbett, the Coastguard Cottages representative on the Committee, offered to *"control the rabbit population discreetly with ferrets and this was accepted."*

Image from - *Google.co.uk*

Saline Lagoon, Cuckmere Haven

Following a site meeting in the summer of 1975 it was reported back to the Management Committee that, *"the land behind the shingle ridge above the high water mark was inspected. This consists of a rectangular area below the level of the surrounding land. It was found to have a quantity of material, mostly metal, dumped in it. It was considered that when the rubbish had been cleared this area could easily be flooded to make an attractive pool for waders and other birds."*

The River Authority was consulted and agreed in principle to some low-lying land in the Cuckmere Estuary being flooded and it was suggested that the Nature Conservancy Council might contribute towards the cost. At the next meeting it was reported that the Southern Water Authority had offered to undertake the flooding so it was agreed that the rubbish would be cleared from the site by the Warden, John Gascoigne, and taken away by Lewes District Council.

It appears that nothing more was done about this project and it is not mentioned in the Minutes again until 1984 when the Management Committee approached the Southern Water Authority, who were carrying out maintenance work on the beach, and requested them to provide a sluice to the low-lying land behind the beach at Cuckmere Haven to create a habitat for wading birds.

Wader Pool
- Photo by Alison Baker

In the summer of 1985, exactly ten years from when the idea was first mooted, it was reported that representations had been made to the Water Authority about completion of the sluice to the land behind the shingle bank; and finally, in January 1986 it was noted that the sluice had been completed and that keys would be obtained.

~ *Saline Lagoon, Cuckmere Haven* ~

Urgent works carried out by the Southern Water Authority in 1990 resulted in the destruction of two species of rare plants (unfortunately not named in the Minutes). The Ranger, Monty Larkin, reported that the correct consultation procedures had been followed but he did not have a copy of the Schedule of Plants which had been produced by the Seaford Natural History Society. Mr Hemingway offered to produce a revised Schedule of Plants to include their location; this offer was accepted with grateful thanks. The following year the Ranger was asked to, *"express the Committee's concern to the National Rivers Authority regarding the large amount of shingle now entering Cuckmere Haven and request details of their proposals for future tipping on the Local Nature Reserve."*

The first Readers Digest Beachwatch, a national event, took place in September 1996 when the beach and the area immediately behind was cleared and approximately 30 bin bags full of rubbish were taken off the reserve. The event was repeated the following September *"and beaches along the Heritage Coast, including Hope Gap and Cuckmere Haven, were cleaned and surveyed by Sussex Downs Conservation Board staff and volunteers along with staff from Readers Digest magazine."*

At a 1999 Management Committee Meeting it was noted that autumn storms and high tides had breached the shingle bank and river bank on both sides of the lower Cuckmere. This had resulted in the loss of rare shingle flora as well as significant damage to sea defences. Further storms over the Christmas period caused more damage and it was subsequently reported that the Environment Agency (EA) had reinstated the shingle bank at the mouth of the Cuckmere River and that they were in the process of replacing groynes, *"so that sediment and shingle can be trapped to replenish the beach."*

The first regular group litter clean by members of the Natural History Society in 2000 had yielded 6 bags of rubbish. The Management Committee agreed

Groynes at Cuckmere Haven
- Photo by Alison Baker

~ Saline Lagoon, Cuckmere Haven ~

to thank the volunteers for their efforts and to diary the 1st Saturday of each month for this. N.B. *This was quickly changed to the first Sunday of each month.*

The following year the Management Committee were informed that major beach reconstruction works had been delayed by recent bad weather but would be completed soon; and in 2003 the Ranger, Simon McHugh, reported that the, *"EA had carried out emergency works in November during very wet weather".*

Cuckmere River Meanders
- Photo by Alison Baker

In 2005 the South Downs Coastal Group Shoreline Management Plan was considered by the Committee. It was agreed that while, historically, coastal land had been reclaimed, the coastline here was generally suffering erosion rather than deposition resulting in a narrower fringe of habitat, but the SHLNRMC recognised the need to defend economic areas and the natural development of the coastline. Jon Curson, English Nature [EN] representative, believed that the salt marsh would establish within 2-5 years following managed realignment. EN would not support any further coastal defences relating to this Plan. It was resolved to support the plan for Cuckmere Haven and the Nature Reserve.

No further mention is contained within the Minutes until 2011 when the February issue of the Cuckmere Estuary Pathfinder Project newsletter containing six options (unfortunately not listed) was discussed. All agreed that the option selected should benefit the Local Nature Reserve and thus not detract from it. It was agreed that Options A, B and C were likely to provide benefits which D, E and F would not. The Committee voted 5 to 2 in favour of options A, B or C. It was further agreed that any changes proposed for access to the Reserve should not compromise the wildness of the Reserve or be detrimental to the wildlife.

In 2013 it was noted that the EA was due to clear the river mouth and rebuild the shingle on the west beach. Work was clearly proceeding on plans for the Cuckmere Estuary because the Coastguard Cottages representative, Michael

~ Saline Lagoon, Cuckmere Haven ~

Ann, reported in 2014 that, *"all the options were considered [by the Estuary Task Group] and it was agreed to keep the river banks as passable rights of way until the successful reactivation of the meanders. This means that four times a month the whole valley will flood which will enable a saltmarsh to establish. When the toxicity of the meanders has been tested and if the earth is deemed suitable this will be used to create islands on the west side of the valley. Even when the valley is flooded the islands will be visible which means they can house a greater number of species."*

N.B. In February 2017 the Management Committee were told by the South Downs National Park Authority representative that, *"further to several meetings of the Cuckmere Estuary Partnership, the proposed scheme to reactivate the meanders ('Option C') is no longer being taken forward........ and that "discussions are on-going with all parties working together to compromise and find consensus on an alternative scheme which honours the key principles of the Pathfinder consultation and finds a feasible way forward."*

Tank traps at the lagoon
- Photo by Alison Baker

Further tension between the Management Committee and the Environment Agency occurred in early 2015 when it was reported that recent shingle work had been carried out with no prior warning and had resulted in part of the saltmarsh being destroyed. The EA representative apologised that Sussex Wildlife Trust [SWT], now managing the site, had not been consulted and noted that the EA are continuing to work with Natural England (NE) to make space for the shingle to be moved to; to try and keep the river mouth clear and stop the shingle circulating round. He confirmed that EA were contemplating doing more work before April and he would speak with SWT and NE to arrange a site meeting. Unfortunately this site meeting did not take place before the Environment Agency carried out the second phase of shingle clearance and yet more shingle was put into the saltmarsh area.

~ Saline Lagoon, Cuckmere Haven ~

The South Downs National Park Volunteer Group took part in two Big Beach Cleans at the saline lagoon and by Hope Gap Steps in 2016 and the Committee were updated on the proposals regarding the movement of shingle down at the river mouth. The National Trust were not keen to have the shingle put on its land behind the tank traps, so the proposal was potentially to have the shingle put on the east side of the river, the exact location yet to be identified. It was noted that this is East Sussex County Council land and parts of it are established vegetative shingle. The Management Committee reiterated their wish to ensure that communication was kept open with regards to the shingle movement as, *"since being dumped in the saline lagoon in the past there is a noticeable decline in the number of invertebrates."*

Shingle being tipped to reinforce the Cuckmere River bank - *Photo by Colin Whiteman, SNHS*

The SDNP Volunteers were back in Cuckmere Haven the following year and focused on beach cleaning the saline lagoon. Exactly what they found in it is not recorded but, *"it was pointed out that some large heavy material, including ropes, is difficult to deal with and requires local authority input."*

The Ranger, Sarah Quantrill, reported that the Environment Agency were due to carry out shingle movement from the mouth of the Cuckmere River in March 2017. This time they would be depositing the shingle near the pillbox on National Trust land but they are still looking at longer term options. SWT confirmed that they would strongly oppose any suggestion to relook at the saline lagoon being a possible option.

The EA did move more shingle in March after which the Ranger reported that, unfortunately, its height would probably cause more shingle to wash into the lagoon and that this really does matter. Too-frequent disturbance to the habitat means that species have too little time to respond and relocate and the quality of the lagoon biodiversity will reduce.

~ Surveys ~

Surveys

Even before the land was designated as a Local Nature Reserve there was documented interest in exactly what species were to be found there.

The original petition for the creation of a Nature Reserve on Seaford Head, probably authored by Mr Hemingway (a founder member of the Natural History Society and a teacher at Blatchington Court School, Seaford), stated in 1966 that, *"from a botanical point of view, the coastal area extending from Seaford Head to Cuckmere Haven and the River Cuckmere inland as far as Exceat Bridge is notable not only for the number of uncommon species which are found there but also for its wide variety of contrasting and relatively undisturbed habitats. As such, it is not only one of the most attractive and unspoilt parts of the Sussex coast but of very great interest to lovers of wild flowers and students of the British flora and a convenient locality to which students and school-children may be taken to learn about a wide range of vegetation types."* Attached to this report was a list of over 260 botanical species recorded as being present in this area.

Round-headed Rampion 'Pride of Sussex'
- Photo by Clare Mayers, SNHS

Extract from first species survey
- Image from Seaford Town Council archives

You will see that as well as the names of the plants, the

~ Surveys ~

environment in which they were found has also been noted i.e. chalk grassland; cliff edges; grassland; waste ground; shingle; salt marsh; ditches/brackish meadows; banks/hedgerows. As far as we know this is the very first systematic species survey of Seaford Head but only records plants; although the original petition also included a list of 26 species of birds compiled from memory by Mr Port, a Brighton-based birder, who noted that *"I don't keep records of the common migrants. The only rarities which I have seen at Hope Gap in the last five or six years were a Tawny Pipit and a party of 4 Ortolan Buntings."*

These records, interesting though they are, are by modern standards not detailed enough (i.e. no grid references, no photographs to ensure positive identification etc.) to be acceptable as an official Reserve record. To make it onto the list nowadays the recording requirements are much more stringent.

Although Mr Hemingway was obviously a plant man, he was also very keen that other species on Seaford Head should be noted. The archive of the Natural History Society in December 1969 notes that he *"said record cards were available for any members willing to record natural history species on the Seaford Head Reserve."*

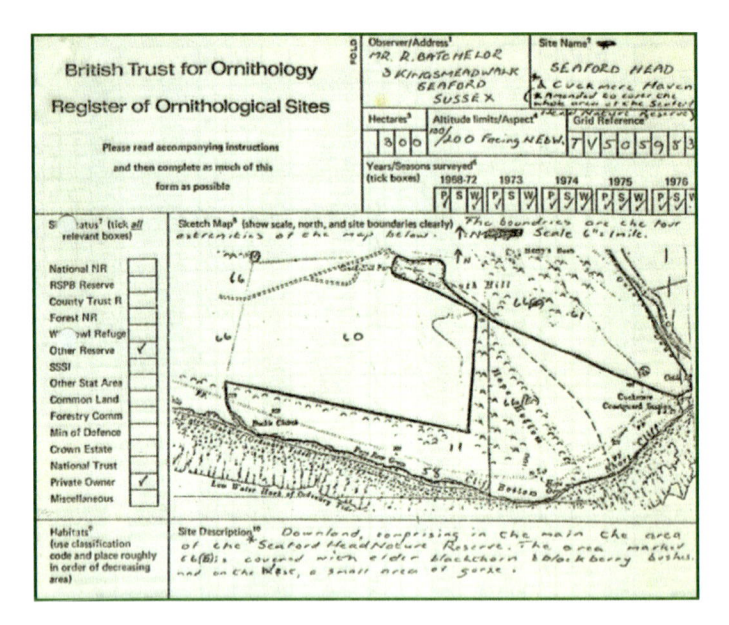

Extract from 1976 BTO survey
- Image from Seaford Town Council archives

At the end of 1974 the Management Committee noted that a survey would be required as part of the information needed to prepare a Management Plan and that *"it was hoped that the Seaford Natural History Society would undertake the necessary work next year."* Mr Hemingway, who was the Society's representative on the Management Committee, *"spoke of work projected on the Seaford Head and Cuckmere Estuary nature reserve; the area to be divided for this purpose into about 20 sections* (see separate section on Land Management)*, and [in January 1975] he asked for volunteers for helping with the survey,"*; and then

~ Surveys ~

again in April *"Mr Hemingway asked for more volunteers to help with survey of Seaford Head nature reserve."*

There is no record that this was done, but in January 1981 a work programme for the year was being prepared and there was *"considerable discussion as to the implementation of this programme so as to ensure that a proper balance of vegetation was maintained to ensure the retention of suitable breeding sites for the various species of birds which at present are found on the Reserve."*

Male Gatekeeper butterfly
- Photo by Paul Baker, SNHS

Despite there being no mention in the Management Committee records of a survey in 1984, the Natural History Society records that *"Mr Hemingway showed the map of the Seaford Head Nature Reserve giving the areas for which plant surveys are to be carried out."* It is doubtful whether much work was actually undertaken because the Management Committee Minutes do record that in 1987 *"a vegetation survey was felt to be urgently needed, and the County Ecologist [now Dr Tait] together with Mr Hemingway were authorised to pay for assistance with this work."* Mr Hemingway again asked the Natural History Society for volunteers to continue the plant survey as *"only 272 species were noted last year and all sections were not covered*."*

In 1986, Chris Lowmass, currently the chair of the Management Committee, undertook a butterfly survey recording 19 different species of butterfly, and an unidentified person added more than 13 different species of moths including the Emperor Moth which is not yet on the current species list for the Reserve. This person also noted the presence of numerous and varied micro-moths, beetles (the Bloody-nosed beetle and the Dor beetle being the most memorable), several species of bumble

Bloody-nosed beetle
- Photo by Paul Baker, SNHS

~ Surveys ~

bees, numerous species of bugs, flies and wasps and an interesting and varied snail population.

By January 1988 Mr Hemingway was able to give the County Ecologist a list of plants which had been compiled by the Seaford Natural History Society, and it was agreed that Dr Tait should undertake the management of a comprehensive survey. Once again Mr Hemingway asked the Natural History Society members for *"more help in listing the plants found in the Seaford Head Reserve. At present 298 plants have been noted*."*

Spring star
- Photo by Chris Brewer, SNHS

The October 1988 edition of The Seaford Naturalist, the newsletter of the Natural History Society, reports on a summer walk meeting which took place in August and was *"planned to be part of the botanical survey of the Nature Reserve at present being provided for the management committee. The dykes were the special target [of the day]*."*

In August 1990 *"a small party [from the Natural History Society] surveyed the area behind Lullington Close and identified a total of 50 plants, 7 grasses and 11 trees and shrubs*."*

It seems that it was not only local organisations who were interested in what was on the Reserve. In 1991 the Management Committee received a botanical (National Vegetation Classification) survey of Seaford Head recently produced by English Nature as part of their comprehensive survey of chalk downland on the South Downs*. The Natural History Society had also been

Common Carder Bee
- Photo by Mike Kerry, SNHS

~ Surveys ~

busy once again and an updated list of flora compiled by members, 332 species, was presented to the Management Committee in 1992.

In the November 1992 issue of The Seaford Naturalist, Mrs Amoore, Secretary to the Natural History Society as well as Chair of the Management Committee, reported that the Moon Carrot, *"at Hope Gap is doing well in spite of the rabbits. As well as the usual places on the sides of the hollow leading down to the sea, it is occurring for the first time on the cliffs to the east. The Park Ranger reports having counted some 500 flowering stems over about six weeks."* She further reported in 1995 that *"the green-veined/winged orchid is flourishing; she had counted 80 flowering spikes on a recent visit to the Reserve."*

Green-winged Orchid
- Photo by Paul Baker, SNHS

In 1996 the Ranger, Paul Ling, reported to the Management committee and drew attention to four species of bee which had been found on the Reserve during a recent survey*, including the Anthophora retusa (Potter Flower-bee), which had been found to be the largest colony in the UK. It was noted that all these species were contained in the Red Data Book of rare species of wildlife.

By October Neil Featherstone had taken over as Ranger and he reported that *"one of the first sightings in Britain of the Philanthus triangulum (Bee Wolf), a species of wasp, had been made on the Reserve."*

The Readers Digest Beachwatch, an annual national event which ran from 1993 to 1999, took place at the end of September 1997 and beaches along the Heritage Coast, including Hope Gap and Cuckmere Haven, were cleaned and surveyed by Sussex Downs Conservation Board staff and volunteers along with staff from Readers Digest magazine*.

A vegetation survey was planned for 1998 as part of the information needed for the new Management Plan. The Ranger suggested that a local surveyor be used to undertake this work and the Management Committee approved this plan. The National Trust suggested that they could help with the cost of the survey and the Ranger was asked to investigate whether any grant aid was available to pay

~ Surveys ~

for this. Neil Featherstone informed the Committee in November 1999 that he had secured funding from English Nature.

The *ad hoc* recording of species on the Reserve tended to just be species of particular interest or rarity; for example there were no recorded sightings of a rabbit or a daisy. Clearly this situation needed to be addressed and by 1999 things were in full swing with an invertebrate and botanical survey under way, as detailed as funds would allow, and a bat survey planned for the summer. The intention was *"to include the whole of the golf course as there are areas of interest that lie outside of the Reserve but within the buffer zone surrounding it".* It was also planned to present the information in the format of a National Vegetation Classification (NVC) Report which would enable the Committee to *"provide detailed prescriptions for the management of the Reserve in the pending review of the Management Plan."*

Adela croesella
- Photo by Colin Whiteman, SNHS

At the end of the year the Management Committee recorded their thanks to various people for surveys on Lepidoptera (moths), Odonata (dragonflies and damselflies), and Orthoptera (grasshoppers and crickets). It was also reported that the Sussex Ornithological Society had begun a survey of bird populations (and migrant birds in particular), and had provided the Committee with 30 years of backdated records of bird sighting in the area, regrettably none of this was found amongst the archives.

Great green bush cricket
- Photo by Clare Mayers, SNHS

~ Surveys ~

Early in 2000 it was noted that a local volunteer had agreed to undertake a bird survey and the Ranger, Fran Southgate, reported that *"a fixed point survey has been set up comprising 18 quadrats covering the various important habitats in the Reserve. I have attempted to make the survey as comprehensive as possible in order to enable it to be carried out easily by volunteers and employees alike – hopefully over a long period of time."* The Committee promptly resolved that *"the information gained from any surveys of flora, fauna and birds on the LNR be submitted to the [Sussex]Biological Record Centre."*

Barred Tooth-striped Moth
- Photo by Clare Mayers, SNHS

Also in 2000 the Ranger reported on the results of the moth survey when 104 species had been recorded over three visits to the Reserve. Members were informed that the Barred Tooth-Striped Moth (Trichopteryx polycommata) had been found at Hope Gap and that this was a biodiversity action plan species identified as an endangered species at the 1992 Rio Summit. A recent check of this data has revealed that 25 species are not on the master list for the Reserve and have now been submitted to the Sussex Biodiversity Records Centre by the Seaford Natural History Society, as the records were made by a respected authority and with sufficient detail to be confident of their locations.

Interest in the Reserve was obviously on the increase as in 2001 the Ranger reported that a local invertebrate expert had offered to conduct a survey on the Reserve, and the Committee agreed to apply for a grant from English Nature so this could be done – obviously successfully as the survey* went ahead a few months later when three Red Data Book (RDB) species, unfortunately not named, were documented by the County

Adder and grass snake
- Photo by Clare Mayers, SNHS

~ Surveys ~

South Hill Barn car park
~ Photo by Alison Baker

Recorder for Beetles (Coleoptera) and Plant Bugs (Heteroptera). So, too, did a mollusc survey* which found 31 species from 10 families, the most notable being Helicella itala which is the subject of a Sussex Species Action Plan. All were found in the area surrounding Hope Gap.

A survey of a different kind was conducted in June 2002 when a survey of users of the South Hill Barn car park was undertaken by Lewes District Council*. The following June when the results of the survey were presented to the Management Committee for comment it was agreed to express their disappointment that the survey had been done during high summer which meant that only 44% of the respondents were local people.

In June 2006 a revised Management Plan was being compiled and the Ranger, Tracey Younghusband, was asked to get quotations for a species survey. It was noted that plant, butterflies, invertebrates, birds, and fungi surveys should start.

In February 2007 it was agreed that some vegetation surveys should be undertaken to ascertain how it is being affected by grazing. Three days were allocated for this, one in March, June and September. In the summer of 2008 it was reported that a survey of peregrine falcons* was being carried out and a breeding pair had been found.

By October 2010 the responsibility for producing a Management Plan had fallen to the South Downs Joint Committee (see separate section on Governance) who advised the Committee of the presence of the very rare solitary Anthophora Retusa (Potter Flower-bee) on the cliff face – probably the same colony recorded in 1996. At the same

Robin
~ Photo by Colin Whiteman, SNHS

~ Surveys ~

meeting it was reported that a rare albino type of butterfly had been found at Hope Gap.

It is safe to assume that the South Downs Joint Committee never did complete their draft Plan in 2010 as it was noted in 2012 that *"the current Management Plan was produced in 2001 and a new draft Management Plan is progressing with surveys and habitat maps being produced [by Sussex Wildlife Trust]. Field work will take place until the end of August to enable all surveys etc. to be done and submission of the draft Plan is expected in Sept 2012."*

Moon Carrot
~ Photo by Alison Baker

The Natural History Society representative, Anne Fletcher, advised the Committee in April 2013 that the Society would be carrying out a survey of the Moon Carrot *(Seseli libanotis)* when the flowers are out in August. This was as a result of a report she had given to the Society that the new Nature Reserve Management Plan recommended a number of annual surveys, including a survey of Moon Carrot. It was agreed that the Society would take responsibility for this and *"it was noted that this year's survey will provide the baseline for future years."*

The Sussex Ornithological Society reported that *"the Common Bird Census will be conducted in spring when the birds are settling.......... The survey will include the plotting of main breeding/ territory birds but also migrant birds."* It was also noted that the Sussex Fish Survey* had taken place in September 2012.

Juvenile Common Shrew
~ Photo by Jack Hobson, grandson

~ Surveys ~

At the end of November 2014 the Committee were informed that a survey of dragonflies*, the second annual Moon Carrot survey and the survey on breeding birds had been done*. It was also reported that *"a bee specialist, has visited the Reserve to see the extremely rare Potter Flower-bee and was very pleased with the habitat management."*

In 2015 the Sussex Wildlife Trust Senior Ecologist, Graeme Lyons, carried out the Invertebrate Assemblage Survey; the annual Common Bird Census was completed as was the Moon Carrot survey, and funding was sought to survey the Potter Flower-bee again.

Regular surveys were definitely becoming the norm and in 2016 the Committee were informed that Invertebrate surveys had been carried out monthly by Sussex Wildlife Trust over the summer with help from the Natural History Society; the annual Moon Carrot survey had been done as had the Common Bird census, carried out for many years by Matt Eade and now handed over to Colin Whiteman, the Natural History Society representative on the Management Committee.

2017 saw the Natural History Society take on the regular surveying of Reptiles and Butterflies on the Reserve as well as the annual Moon Carrot survey (see table opposite), and it was reported that a very popular Moth Evening had been held during the school holidays in August. That occasion was very successful with the leader of the event writing afterwards, *"The good news is that we saw what could have been the greatest number of Barred Tooth-striped moths recorded at one site, at least in the modern era.......... It might be that Hope Bottom is the best UK site for this species."* Also in 2017 it was noted that the National Trust planned to resurvey the section of the grazed area in their portion of the Reserve, part of the agricultural tenancy, last carried out in 1994.

The number of individual Moon Carrot plants recorded in each transect, as illustrated in the image on the left, are shown in the following table:

~ Surveys ~

Transect	\multicolumn{6}{c}{NUMBER OF MOON CARROT PLANTS}
	2013	2014	2015	2016	2017	2018
1	65	31	155	135	257	540
2	86	105	364	370	456	1226
3	187	138	594	330	378	564
4	124	87	375	265	276	543
5	207	135	498	118	78	
6	139	39	138	29	1	-
7	26	4	4	22	0	-
8	46	34	44		6	-
9	22	21				1
TOTAL	902	594	2172	1269	1452	2874

2017 also saw the Natural History Society representative, Colin Whiteman, report to the Management Committee that, *"Reptile monitoring continues with up to eight adders present during one monitoring circuit, along with a number of lizards and the first slow worms and grass snake records for the Reserve. So far this year 32 new species have been added to SHLNR list and more are in the pipeline, having been forwarded to the Sussex Biodiversity Record Centre. This is helping SHLNR to move towards the top ten nature reserves in Sussex for species numbers, as defined by SWT, a challenge set by Graeme Lyons, SWT Senior Ecologist."*

An article written by Natural History Society members for the Adastra magazine (an annual review of wildlife recording in Sussex) reports, *"beginning in 2015 we established a project of monitoring, on a weekly basis, the flora and fauna of two ride-side scallops cleared of scrub by SWT working parties. This helped in understanding the benefits to wildlife of the scrub control, which has been a feature of work across the reserve. The scallop monitoring revealed 43 positively*

Ornate Shieldbug
- Photo by Colin Whiteman, SNHS

~ Surveys ~

Sowerbyella radiculata
- Photo by Jim Howell, SNHS

identified new reserve species in 2015 of which the Ornate Shieldbug (*Eurydema ornata*), only the second recorded in Sussex, was the highlight."

For the past few years the Natural History Society have also undertaken annual counts of Twayblade (a spring flowering orchid), Green-winged Orchids and Autumn Ladies Tresses within the Reserve, none of them common but present here.

The Natural History Society was privileged to host the Sussex Fungi Group on a recording visit in October 2017. Amongst the fungi recorded were Sowerbyella radiculata, Perenniporia ochroleuca and Entoloma pseudoturci, all of which were new to all SWT Reserves. There was great excitement when Lepiota cf. andegavensis, was spotted as it had not been identified in the UK before.

Weekly butterfly recording began in 2017 with volunteers walking two different routes (or transects) on the Reserve; a 'practice season' before the official registration of the routes with the Butterfly Conservation Trust for 2018 and beyond. Flight patterns from observations of some common species during the 2017 survey are shown in the table below:

	May	June	July	August	Sept	Oct
Comma						
Common Blue						
Gatekeeper						
Large Skipper						
Red Admiral						
Small Copper						
Small Heath						
Small Skipper						

0	>0 to 5	>5 to 10	>10 to 25	>25 to 50	over 50

Key: Percentage of each species seen in each week
Analysis kindly supplied by Paul Chalmers-Dickson

~ Surveys ~

In early 2017, Seaford Natural History Society produced a list of all the species ever recorded on the whole of the Reserve; this data was taken from official Sussex Biodiversity Record Centre records, which are updated twice a year. This corresponds to an official master list of species recorded in the Sussex Wildlife Trust section of the Reserve, which has been produced annually by the SWT Senior Ecologist, Graeme Lyons, since 2017.

Chaffinch
- Photo by Colin Whiteman, SNHS

At the beginning of 2018 the master list of species recorded as being present on the SWT-managed section of the Reserve stood at 1,498, an increase of 140 over the previous year. The surveys conducted by the Natural History Society, solely on the SWT-managed section, (which does not include the golf course or the farmland) during 2017 are not part of those figures and should add significantly to that list. The Natural History Society figure for the whole Reserve which does include the National Trust section and the foreshore is 1,803, including a surprisingly large number of Biodiversity Action Plan and/or Red Data Book species (species of conservation concern), including, in addition to those mentioned in the text above, Yellowhammer (bird); Common European Viper, Yellow-footed Mining bee; Cladonia Convoluta, a lichen not recorded since 1994, and going back even further a Little Bustard logged in 1846.

Having just completed the 2019 master list, Graeme Lyons noted in a Facebook post: *"Although Seaford Head has only just passed over the 1,000 species of invertebrate (1008 which is ranked 9th out of 32 Sussex Wildlife Trust sites), the proportion of rare or scarce species is 12.8%. This is ranked third after Rye Harbour (14.8%) and Iping Common (13.9%). This also means it has the highest proportion of rare or scarce inverts on any of our [SWT] chalk-grassland sites."*

> **If you would like to become involved in the Natural History Society surveying work on Seaford Head you can find out more at:**
> **www.seafordnaturalhistory.org.uk/**

** indicates reports/data **not** found amongst the available archive material*

Artichoke Peace Camp

While the Olympics were taking place in London in 2012 something out-of-the-ordinary was taking place in the Local Nature Reserve.

In February 2012 the Management Committee were approached by the organisers of the project for permission to hold a *"peace camp in the 'Memorial Field' at Cuckmere, one of a number of events to be held nationwide"*. The encampment would consist of hundreds of small illuminated tents forming a subtle glowing effect, and up to 20 people would be staffing the site for a week. It was noted that Natural England would need to be consulted because the event could have a detrimental effect on the SSSI.

Permission was obviously given, and quite quickly too, because in June it was reported that the camp would be situated next to the Canadian Memorial. Restrictions such as timed ticketing, no vehicles and protective matting if the weather should be bad were in place. But what exactly was happening?

In the words of the organisers, taken from their website, *"Eight murmuring, glowing encampments appeared simultaneously at some of the UK's most beautiful and remote coastal locations, from County Antrim to the tip of Cornwall, from the Isle of Lewis to the Sussex Cliffs. Designed to be visited between dusk and dawn, Peace Camp was a poignant exploration of love poetry and a celebration of the extraordinary variety and beauty of our coastline."*

At the November Management Committee meeting the Coastguard Cottages representative reported that over 1,000 people had visited the camp, there were no disturbances, and the impact on the ground was minimal and had since recovered.

Peace Camp at Cuckmere Haven, East Sussex July 2012
*- Copyright is Benedict Johnson
From: www.artichoke.uk.com/project/peace-camp*

~ Canadian War Memorial ~

Canadian War Memorial

In October 2005 it was reported to the Management Committee that a local resident, Leslie Edwards, had recently died and one of the things he saw during his lifetime was an attack on Canadian troops stationed in the field opposite the Coastguard Cottages. Cuckmere Haven was considered to be a likely enemy landing site in the event of a German invasion. According to Mr Edwards these troops were strafed by German fighter aircraft during the Battle of Britain in 1940 and many were killed. It had been suggested that a commemorative plaque be erected describing what happened and also remembering Mr Edwards. This information was received in good faith and it was agreed that Carolyn McCourt, the Coastguard Cottages representative on the Committee, be asked to draw up a design for the plaque and that a possible location would be investigated at the next site meeting. The British Legion would be invited to attend and the local historic society would be contacted to ensure that the information was not lost and also be invited to attend the site visit.

Canadian War Memorial
- Photo by Paul Baker, SNHS

By June 2006 the site visit had taken place and representatives from the Royal British Legion (RBL) and the local museum had met with Committee members to discuss this proposal. It was noted that the late Mr Edwards used to place flowers on the site on Remembrance Day. Ms McCourt was invited to read her suggested wording for the memorial plaque which was thought to be most appropriate (see overleaf). It was agreed that the plaque should be plain apart from the wording and that it would be mounted on a flint pedestal facing west slightly away from the western boundary of the area. The brass plaque had been

~ Canadian War Memorial ~

priced at £545 plus VAT but the cost of pedestal was not yet known. When full costings had been received contributions would be sought from the RBL and the Canadian Veterans Association. It was further agreed that the RBL, the Canadian Veterans Association and the Canadian High Commissioner would be invited to the opening ceremony.

At the October meeting it was reported that the Seaford Branch of the RBL and the Canadian Veterans Association had been approached for donations towards the cost of the memorial as well as being invited to the dedication ceremony. A sketch of the memorial was circulated and it was noted that the plaque would be A3 in size and that work had already started. There is no record of the total cost but it was noted that the Canadian Veterans Association had donated £400 towards the project.

The Minutes of February 2007 recorded that *"the Dedication Service on 20th Nov was a great success. The rain held off and everyone seemed to enjoy the refreshments at the RBL afterwards."*

THIS PLAQUE COMMEMORATES THE SOLDIERS WHO DIED IN THIS AREA AND SPECIFICALLY IN THIS FIELD DURING WORLD WAR 2. THEIR NUMBERS ARE UNKNOWN BUT THEIR MEMORY LIVES ON. THE FOLLOWING IS A PERSONAL TESTIMONY FROM CORPORAL LESLIE EDWARDS (1920-2004), A LOCAL MAN WHO SERVED IN THE AREA AND LAID POPPIES ON THIS SPOT EVERY REMEMBRANCE DAY UNTIL HIS DEATH.

"I WILL NEVER FORGET THE DAY IN 1940 WHEN A CANADIAN COMPANY CAME TO CUCKMERE AND PITCHED THEIR TENTS IN THIS FIELD. I WAS STATIONED HERE AND KNEW THAT BOMBERS REGULARLY USED THIS VALLEY FOR NAVIGATION PURPOSES. I TRIED TO TELL THE COMMANDING OFFICER BUT HE WAS NOT INTERESTED IN WHAT I HAD TO SAY. TWO MORNINGS LATER THE MESSERSCHMITT'S ARRIVED. JUST AS THE SUN WAS RISING THEY CAME SKIMMING OVER THE WATER AND UP THE VALLEY. AROUND ALFRISTON THEY BANKED HARD AND CAME BACK. BEARING DOWN ON THE TENTS THEY OPENED FIRE. STEAM, SOIL AND GRASS ROSE IN FRONT OF THEM AS BULLETS AND BOMBS ENTERED THE GROUND. ALL THE YOUNG MEN IN THE MARQUEES AND BELL TENTS WERE KILLED. THE COMMANDING OFFICER, WHO WAS SHAVING AT THE TIME IN THE MIDDLE COASTGUARD COTTAGE, DIED INSTANTLY WHEN A SHELL WENT THROUGH THE WALL THAT HELD HIS MIRROR."

*"Remember me when I am gone away,
Gone far away into the silent land."*
Christina Rossetti

Wording on the Canadian War Memorial plaque

~ *Canadian War Memorial* ~

N.B. There is some disagreement about the historical accuracy of the inscription on this Memorial and various historians, both military and local, have done much research into this event, all of which have been inconclusive. Another plaque is to be erected by the Management Committee stating that Mr Edwards' testimony is officially unverified; and at the same time commemorate all service personnel who were killed at or over Cuckmere Haven during the last war.

―――――――◇◇◇◇◇◇◇―――――――

Civil Aviation Beacon

The first mention of the Civil Aviation Beacon is contained in a Register of Documents 'sealed' (a wax seal of approval) by Seaford Urban District Council, dated March 1952, which granted a *"lease for the Seaford Radio Station (Fan Marker Beacon Site) on Seaford Head to the Minister of Civil Aviation."* Eight years later, in an agreement still filed in the Seaford Town Council archives, permission was granted to the General Post Office (the forerunner of British Telecom) to lay 1,137 yards (1040 metres) of underground cable from Chyngton Road to the VOR (VHF Omni-Directional Radio) station. Any aircraft equipped with a receiving unit is able to determine their position and stay on course by receiving very high frequency (VHF) radio signals transmitted by a network of ground based radio beacons.

The next reference is not until 1973 when a planning application was made for *"redevelopment of existing Radio Navigation Beacon."* The application was submitted in March and approved by May, but there is no record of what these works actually were.

Following the establishment of the Civil Aviation Authority (CAA)[now National Air Traffic Services] in 1972, the Department of Trade subsequently issued the Civil Aviation (Seaford Head) (Creation of Easements and Other Rights Over Land) Order 1975, giving themselves permission to use the land.

Civil Aviation Beacon
- Photo by Paul Baker, SNHS

By 1983 an upgrade was needed. Technology had improved and an application was made to Lewes District Council, who in turn consulted with the Management Committee, to consider an application from the Civil Aviation Authority to convert the existing VOR aircraft navigation aid at Seaford Head to DVOR status. The D stands for Doppler and it enables the identifying code of a navigation beacon to be encrypted.

~ Civil Aviation Beacon ~

The Minutes of that meeting state: *"A plan showing the location of the proposed installation and the sites of two 37ft monitor masts had been circulated to Members, together with an elevation drawing of the DVOR installation. It was intended that this facility should replace the existing installation and would comprise a fenced concrete compound 12m x 10m upon which would be constructed a cabin measuring 8.5m x 3m. The compound would be surrounded by a fence and the whole surmounted by circular decking 30m in diameter upon which would be mounted an aerial array, the central mast of which would stand 8.8m above ground level. The site plan also showed a proposed 3m wide access track of unspecified construction linking the installation with the existing concrete roadway.*

It was resolved:

1. *That the Lewes District Council be thanked for its courtesy in giving this Committee an opportunity to comment upon the application;*

2. *That the Lewes District Council be informed that this Committee does not favour the siting of such a station in this locality for the following reasons:-*

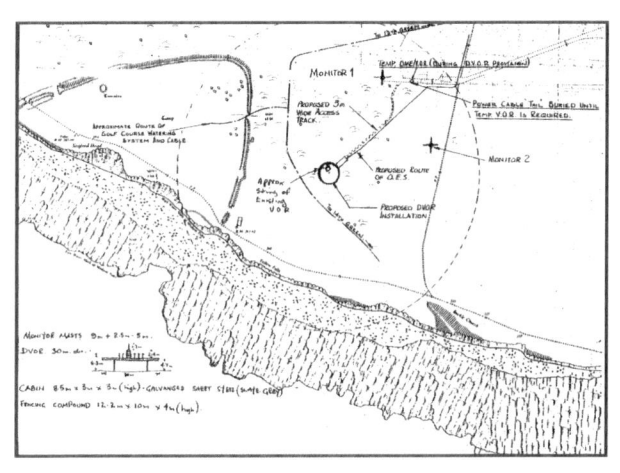

1983 planning application for DVOR upgrade
~ Image from Seaford Town Council archives

   a) *The site is within compartment 13a of this local nature reserve, which forms part of an area of land incorporated in the Reserve in 1978 because of its special interests. Historically the habitat of this compartment supported a number of interesting plants which grew in profusion. In more recent years, however, their numbers had decreased until they were in danger of disappearing entirely. The incorporation of this area into the Reserve and the subsequent management of the land has increased the numbers of these plants and they are now becoming re-established;*

   b) *the compartment includes a habitat particularly suited to the nesting habits of an extremely rare bird which is, at present, in the area;*

c) It is considered that the construction of this station and its associated monitors would seriously interfere with both plant and bird life in the compartment. In addition the construction of any new access road or any extension to the present service road is regarded as being highly undesirable and to be resisted on the grounds that such work and the subsequent use of the access would constitute yet a further intrusion into an area of land which is not only part of the South Downs Area of Outstanding Natural Beauty, but, more importantly, an Area of Special Scientific Interest.

3. That the Lewes District Council be urged to request the Civil Aviation Authority to investigate the possibility of this navigational aid being sited elsewhere in the area where it will have a lesser impact upon the flora and fauna of the coastal downland."

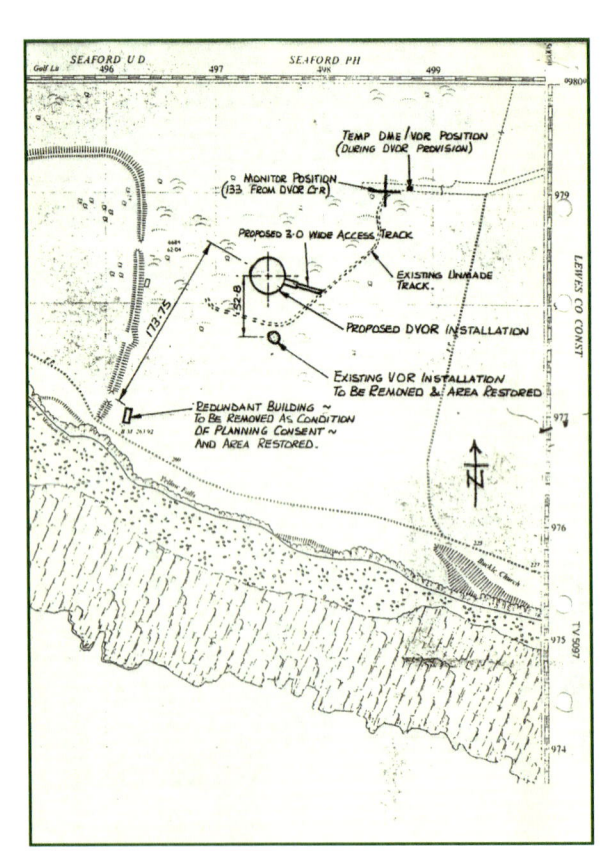

1985 revised planning application
~ Image from Seaford Town Council archives.

This detailed response obviously had some effect because it was another two years before *"the CAA Estates Surveyor produced plans and explained the application and the linkage of the site to the existing concrete roadway. It was resolved that since the new application was less detrimental than the one made in 1983 it was now acceptable providing particularly sensitive areas nearby were avoided."*

There still seemed to be no hurry about this, because it was two years before the Management Committee were requesting the Director of Planning at Lewes District Council to inform them *"of the present position concerning this work as there was concern about the extent of the installation and the size of the working area."* At the end of 1987 it was noted that the contractors engaged on the construction work had agreed to restore the land, and early in 1988 it was further noted that the replanting of the downland surrounding the DVOR installation was progressing satisfactorily.

Unfortunately just a year later it was reported that there had been a number of failures in the scrub replanting around the new DVOR site but that the CAA had provided 60 replacement trees which would be planted this year; and the following year it was agreed that a further 30 hawthorn bushes would be planted at the DVOR site.

More recently, some repair work was undertaken on the beacon in 2015 and it was noted, in response to a query from a Member of the Management Committee, that Natural England had also been consulted and had approved the scrub clearance work which was undertaken in order to allow access to the equipment.

~ Country Club Proposal ~

Country Club Proposal

In the Minutes of the Seaford Sub-committee of October 1979, Lewes District Council were presented with draft proposals for two additional golf courses, an equestrian centre, a leisure centre, a hotel and residential accommodation on 570 acres of land on Seaford Head, most of it within the Local Nature Reserve (see map). Staggeringly the Committee were sufficiently interested in this scheme to authorise planning officers to make further enquiries, even though it was noted that it was contrary to existing agreements under the Town and Country Planning Act and would need the approval of East Sussex County Council, Nature Conservancy Council, the Seaford Head Local Nature Reserve Management Committee and last, but not least, the Secretary of State. There is no further mention of this scheme so presumably it was withdrawn.

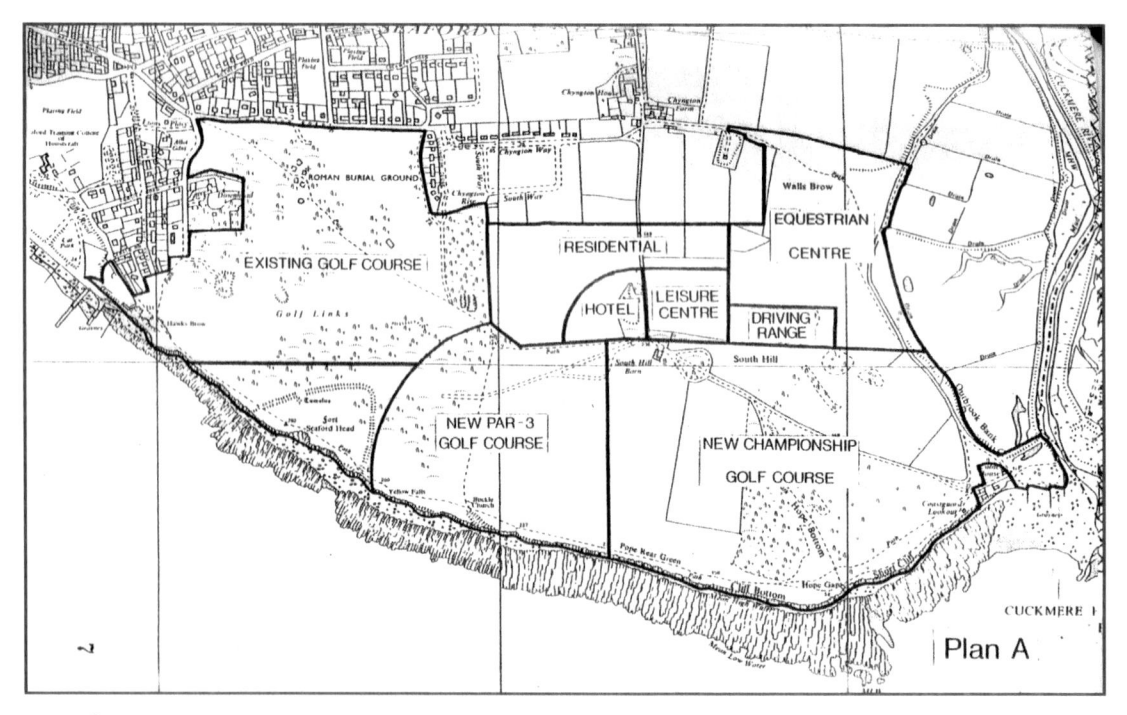

Map from Lewes District Council archives 1979
- Courtesy of The Keep, Brighton, showing the proposed country club layout on Seaford Head

~ Drones ~

Drones

Drones were the 'must-have' Christmas presents of 2014 and it was soon being brought to the attention of the Management Committee that these were being flown in the Reserve. It was noted that operators of this type of equipment must be regulated by the Civil Aviation Authority in order to have the necessary insurance. It was further noted that Lewes District Council have no bye-laws in place prohibiting the use of drones or model airplanes and a discussion took place as to whether one should be created. The Committee were informed that the National Trust have a blanket ban on model airplanes and drones on their land.

By the summer it was being reported that drones were being used for filming, which could be controlled, but public usage was increasing and there was a risk that this would disturb nesting birds and it was agreed that the Reserve's bye-laws, the SSSI Regulations and the Civil Aviation Authority's website would be consulted for guidance.

- Photo by Mike Kerry, SNHS

It was stressed that a blanket ban on the use of drones was not desirable as they were sometimes used as part of a filming contract and would be also be a useful way for Sussex Wildlife Trust to carry out surveys of the Reserve. It was agreed that some signage regarding unauthorised use was required. A report from the Natural History Society representative, Colin Whiteman, in June 2016 stated that there were at least three Fulmar nests in the cliffs between Hope Gap Steps and the Coastguard Cottages which would be particularly susceptible to the potential damage and disruption that drones could cause.

~ *Filming* ~

Filming

Seaford Head Nature Reserve with the spectacular backdrop of the Coastguard Cottages framed by the Seven Sisters cliffs and the glorious unspoilt beaches at Cuckmere Haven and Hope Gap are much loved locations for all sorts of artistic projects including films and photo-shoots. The most famous and significant to date being Atonement in 2007 where the lower Cottage featured throughout the film and the hero, played by James McAvoy, died clasping a postcard of the Coastguard Cottages in his hand.

Although not within the Local Nature Reserve, the Coastguard Cottages and Cable Hut are surrounded by it and are an important local landmark. The Cuckmere Haven Coastguard Station was built in 1823 replacing an earlier barrack block which had been constructed to house men from the Customs and Revenue Services working for the Coastal Blockade (or Preventative) Service,

Cuckmere Coastguard Station 1914
- Image courtesy of Seaford Museum & Heritage Society

an attempt to combat smuggling prevalent before, during and after the Napoleonic War. It comprised of the lower Officer's House and the upper two dwellings which housed the Coastguards and their families. The Cable Hut is one of the few remaining cable stations that lined the coast in the early 1900's. It served as an important cable route, receiving messages via overhead wires from London which were then converted to submarine cables, boosted, and sent on to continental Europe and beyond. The Coastguard Station was requisitioned for use by the army in 1914 when a radio mast was installed and remained an active station up until the end of the 1920's.

The Cottages, as cottages – not part of a Coastguard Station, appear in the Chichester Estates sale particulars of 1927, [see section on Land Acquisition] when they were purchased by Mr R Smelt. Mr Smelt's daughter married the son of Mr J Ayres, the last remaining Coastguard Officer, and relatives of the original

~ *Filming* ~

Coastguards still own some of the Cottages. They were commandeered during the Second World War, as Cuckmere Haven beach was heavily fortified against invasion, and used as a decoy for bombers aiming for Newhaven.

The Seven Sisters with these historic Coastguard Cottages in the foreground have become one of the best loved and most famous images in the world. In February 2019 it was voted Britain's favourite view in a Daily Mail survey hosted by Ben Fogle. However, unless a current campaign to maintain the Cottages' sea defence system is successful the future of the Cottages will be uncertain. Surprisingly, the large sea wall built in 1947, and the adjoining lower wall, built in 1987, was funded and has been maintained ever since by the owners of the Cottages and the Cable Hut. Regrettably the Government policy of managed coastal retreat has meant that the Environment Agency has now ceased maintenance of its own sea defences, which adjoin those of the Cottages, and the owners are applying for planning permission to maintain all current defences and continue to protect their Cottages from the ravages of coastal erosion.

If you would like to know more please see the Cuckmere Haven SOS website: http://www.cuckmerehavensos.org/cuckmere-haven-the-cottages

The beauty of the spot continues to draw visitors and film crews alike and, *"Negotiating with film/TV location managers, haggling over the fee; on the day while minding them, the often terrific food, all prepared on site!"* are some of the memorable moments shared by Monty Larkin, Warden 1986 – 1993. Simon McHugh, Ranger 2001 – 2005, recalls, *"we had a film shoot for [the] 'Greenwing' comedy series where they dangled an ambulance over the cliff edge as I watched terrified that it was going to come loose and fall to the sea below, thankfully it didn't!"*

Fees from projects like these, (see Appendix 3), provided a vital source of income for the Management Committee from its inception until 1994 when the Sussex Downs Conservation Board took over responsibility for the site and the filming fees. A grant was then provided by Lewes District Council for funding work on the Reserve until the land was handed back to Seaford Town Council in 2005. The Town Council now retain the filming fees and pay the Sussex Wildlife Trust for their work on the Reserve [see separate section on Governance].

~ Foreshore ~

Foreshore

A local newspaper article (from the Argus?) reported in 1979 that two tons of periwinkles had been illegally taken from the foreshore at Cuckmere Haven during the recent four-month closed season and that 15 warning notices were to be erected. The local Fisheries Officer for the Ministry for Agriculture, Fisheries and Food (MAFF), Jim Howell, said at the time that *"because Cuckmere Haven is a nature reserve one would not have expected people turning up there taking away periwinkles by the hundredweight."*

Foreshore at Hope Gap
- Photo by Alison Baker

At a meeting in 1981 the Management Committee were told that shellfish were again being taken in commercial numbers from the foreshore at Hope Gap and Cuckmere Haven and stocks were much depleted. It was agreed that the bye-law forbidding such activity should be displayed prominently at that location.

This action appears to have sufficed for a while as it was January 1990 before it was reported that large amounts of shellfish were being collected along the foreshore. The Committee expressed their concern, not only at the damage to the environment but also that these molluscs needed sterilising before consumption. It was agreed that the Lewes District Council Environmental Health Department should be contacted for advice.

At the Management Committee AGM in October Lewes District Council (LDC) submitted a report on the potential dangers of human consumption of shellfish taken from the foreshore. The Committee were clearly very concerned about this issue and resolved to ask the Secretary to look into whether the bye-laws could be extended to prevent the taking of crustaceans.

~ Foreshore ~

In the meantime LDC would be asked to *"re-erect the notices:*

a) *warning people of the dangers;*

b) *informing them of the 'closed' season dates when it is illegal to take shellfish; and*

c) *informing them that any shellfish taken are eaten at their own risk".*

This illicit activity brings us seamlessly to the legal situation with regard to the foreshore which, by 1981, had been part of the Local Nature Reserve for 12 years.

The Seaford Urban District Council had first entered into a regulating Lease with the Commissioners of Crown Lands in 1953 to give them the necessary authority to levy charges for fishing boats etc. being pulled up on the beach in Seaford Bay. This Lease was renewed in 1967 and was still in force when the Council was disbanded and the assets transferred to Lewes District Council in 1974. There is no record of when this lease expired but it seems likely to have to have been 1983 (2 x 15-year leases).

In 1978 the Management Committee proposed an extension to the Reserve part of which included the foreshore between the high and low water marks. The Crown Estates Commissioners (formerly the Commissioners of Crown Lands) had no objection to the declaration being made and agreed the draft bye-law in accordance with Clause IVc of the regulating lease held now by Lewes District Council. On the 18th December 1978 Lewes DC dutifully declared that *"all that land comprising the beach and so much of the foreshore as lies between the low water and high water marks of ordinary tides between the eastern boundary of the earth works at Seaford Head and the eastern boundary of the district at Cuckmere Haven containing approximately 26.5 acres"* be managed as a Nature Reserve in accordance with Sections 19 and 21 of the National Parks and Access to the Countryside Act 1949 (see map on page 101).

In 1989 it was reported that Lewes District Council would shortly be considering whether it wished to take a regulating lease of the foreshore from the Crown Estate Commissioners. It was agreed that LDC be informed that *"so far as the foreshore abutting this Nature Reserve is concerned the Committee urges the Council to accept such a regulating lease as a further means of exercising local control over the coastal environment".*

~ Foreshore ~

Actually it is a requirement of establishing a Local Nature Reserve (LNR) that the area involved is owned or leased by a 'local governing body', in this case Lewes District Council. This would mean that without a lease on the foreshore, the ownership would revert to the Crown and it could, presumably, no longer be part of the LNR, or certainly not under local control.

Since Lewes District Council was instrumental in establishing the foreshore as part of the reserve in 1978 with the specific purpose of recognising the foreshore as an integral and biologically important part of the Reserve, and was represented on the LNR Management Committee, it must have been with some relief when later the same year it was reported that *"the Leisure Services Committee of Lewes District Council had now considered this matter and had authorised officers to open negotiations with the Crown Estate Commissioners to a lease of the foreshore between the Martello Tower and the District Boundary at Cuckmere Haven."*

Foreshore at Cuckmere Haven
- Photo by Colin Whiteman, SNHS

In 1991 it was noted that the bye-laws could be extended to prevent the taking of shellfish from the foreshore once the lease of the foreshore had been received from the Crown Estate Commissioners. It was agreed to request that Lewes District Council expedite this lease as soon as possible *"as there is now large-scale taking of shellfish for commercial purposes"*.

This was obviously done since The Crown Estates (formerly the Crown Estates Commissioners) have a record of the foreshore being leased in 1991 but it appears to have been 1995 before the District Council officially informed the Management Committee that they had indeed obtained a regulating lease relating to the foreshore between The Buckle, Seaford and Cuckmere Haven.

This lease was renewed in 1996 and expired in 2016. It has yet to be renewed and the logical body to do this would be Seaford Town Council as owners of the land, although in practice any organisation The Crown Estates felt was suitable could negotiate with to them renew the lease and thus regularise the situation. Regrettably the status of the foreshore within the Local Nature Reserve is currently very uncertain.

~ Foreshore ~

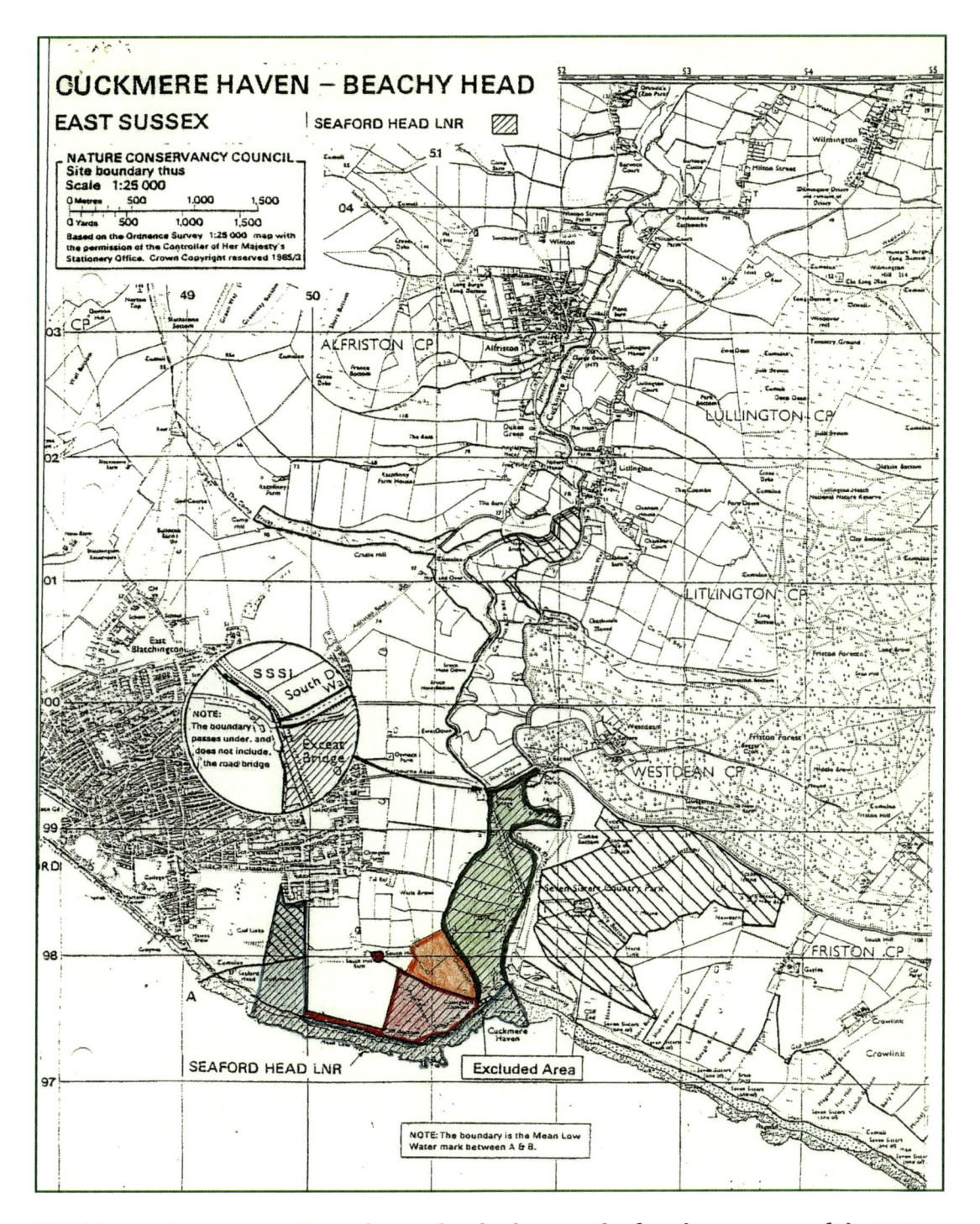

1985 Nature Conservancy Council map clearly showing the foreshore as part of the LNR
- (N.B. The 'excluded area' referred to on the map are the Coastguard Cottages and gardens which are not part of the Reserve). Image from Seaford Town Council archives

Oil Pollution

The English Channel is one of the busiest waterways in the world and in 1981 a recent incident of oil pollution in Seaford Bay was discussed by the Management Committee when it was agreed to share their concerns about the foreshore with the Oil Pollution Officer. A couple of months later it was reported that Lewes District Council were revising their procedures for dealing with oil pollution and flooding, a copy to be supplied to the Warden, John Gascoigne, so that appropriate contact could be made should an oil spill be detected.

It was noted that this did not include pollution of tidal rivers and it was agreed to contact the Southern Water Authority *"to ascertain what measures are proposed in the event of the River Cuckmere being contaminated."* The response appears to have been that a boom would be used in the event of any threat to the River Cuckmere, but no details were available as to what

The 'Leopard' pictured in the early 1980's
- Image from www.hhvferry.com

would be done with it, so further clarification was sought. Nearly a year after their first enquiries the Management Committee were finally in possession of a report detailing the type and the exact siting of this boom in the event of any incident; but it was agreed to make further representation to the Water Authority about the siting of the boom as it was felt that the proposed site was unlikely to protect the valuable salt marsh. Some additional information was received just before the end of 1982 but there is no record what this was.

In January 1983 the County Ecologist reported that a tanker had been lost overboard from the P&O ferry 'Leopard' and washed ashore below Seaford Head.

~ Oil Pollution ~

Lewes District Council and the Police had said the tanker's contents were not harmful but he had information that the tanker contained lubricating oil with an additive which posed a potential hazard to the flora and fauna of the Reserve, particularly if the River Cuckmere and its salt marshes were contaminated. The Committee resolved to convey their concern about the situation to Lewes District Council and the Southern Water Authority.

This subject did not appear in the Minutes again until 1994 when it was agreed that the oil warning sign at the top of Hope Gap steps should be removed.

One-offs – Unexpected Treasure

From the Seaford Head Local Nature Reserve Management Committee Minutes – A Chronological List of the Quirky, Unusual and Otherwise Unexpected!

1972: The Junior section of the Sussex Ornithological Society requested permission to provide artificial nesting sites for Wheatears on the Reserve. Potential locations were discussed and a site meeting was arranged. There is no further mention of this – so did it happen or not?

1978: The Coastguard Observation tower was demolished.

1980: Wild Mink were reported on the Reserve and the Management Committee asked the Ranger, Monty Larkin, to assess numbers. Again, there is no further mention in the Minutes.

1981: Was the International Year of Disabled People and the Management Committee asked Lewes District Council to improve the pedestrian access at South Hill Barn to allow for easy access by wheelchair users.

1983: The Management Committee were informed that Lewes District Council had approved a small archaeological dig to take place in the east bank of the Iron Age camp on Seaford Head but were assured that this would pose no danger to the flora and fauna of the Reserve.

1983: The Management Committee were also informed that Lewes District Council had approved a seismic survey to be undertaken across the eastern part of the Reserve but again were assured that this would pose no danger to the flora and fauna of the Reserve.

~ One-offs – Unexpected Treasure ~

1984: After vandalism to the Praise Plaque in the North-West corner of the Reserve, The Sisterhood of Mary had applied to Lewes DC to provide a replacement. The Management Committee informed Lewes DC that they were not in favour of a replacement on the site.
N.B. An entry in Lewes District Council Minutes, dated 1st December 1969, records a request from the English Sisters of Mary to place a plaque into stone or concrete near the footpath from South Hill Barn to Cuckmere Haven. This was approved subject to siting and construction agreements. Was this the same plaque?

1996: Bicycle parking rings were fixed on the wall adjacent to South Hill Barn. Local cycling clubs to be informed about the new facilities.

1996: £25 had been received from Seaford Head Community College following a Parent Teacher Association (PTA) fun run event through the Reserve.

1997: After much objection, consultation and discussion it had been agreed that the new Sustrans Cycle Route between Chyngton Farm and Exceat would not go through the Reserve after all.

2000: A request had been received from 12 overseas students from the Concordia Group (a Group which had helped pull Ragwort the previous year) to undertake some more voluntary work on the Reserve. This was agreed and a contribution was made towards the cost of their accommodation and refreshments.

2001: The Management Committee received a letter from the Secretary of the East Blatchington Pond Committee asking whether its assets could be transferred to the Committee if it should ever cease to exist. The assets in question were monies and investments which would be donated to Seaford Head. The Management Committee, of course, agreed to the request.

~ One-offs – Unexpected Treasure ~

2003: A request for consent to exchange 'personal vows' following a wedding service held elsewhere had been received. Approximately 20 people were expected to attend on an area just uphill from the coastguard cottages. This was approved. Sadly there is no further mention in the Minutes.

2003: The Ranger, Simon McHugh, reported having been approached by a professional photographer, writing an article for the Shooting Times, who wanted to photograph a local man ferreting on the Reserve. The request was declined.

2003: It was agreed that Seaford Lifeguards be permitted to make occasional use of the crossing through the Reserve to access the lifebuoys in the Cuckmere Haven area.

2005: The Ranger was requested to install hedgehog ramps in the two cattle grids.

2009: It was reported that the Reserve had been used by the English Democrats for their European Election broadcast. Neither the Chairman nor the Ranger had any prior knowledge of this. The Hon. Treasurer was asked to look into the matter but what the outcome was is not recorded.

2010: Councillor (Bob) Brown advised that a rare albino type of butterfly had been found at Hope Gap in September.

2010: Councillor Brown noted that the Vanguard Group were very impressed with the signage along the Vanguard Way. [This long distance footpath stretches from Newhaven Town Railway Station to East Croydon Railway Station, a total of 66 miles, passing through the Reserve on the cliff top at Seaford Head to Hope Gap and the Coastguard Cottages and then along the footpath from there to the Cuckmere Inn].

2013: Chris Lowmass, Chairman, reported that three Red Kites had been seen over Seaford and Friston forest.

2016: Permission for the Archaeological Community Dig on the Reserve planned by Luke Barber was granted. Unfortunately, however, the funding fell through although they were able to dig a research trench and made some good finds including toothbrushes used by soldiers during World War I, cap badges, bullets and similar finds.

~ One-offs – Unexpected Treasure ~

2017: Sarah Quantrill recalls *"On one of our volunteer task days we were again in Hope Gap when we heard music. I firstly thought it was someone being inconsiderate and playing their music loudly on the way to the beach. But along the path came an oxen and a Hari Krishna group, singing and ringing bells. They were doing a peace walk from Eastbourne to Brighton. They gave out lollipops and blessings."*

Eastbourne to Brighton Peace Walk
- Photo by Sarah Quantrill, SWT

2018: Last, but by no means least, is the voyage of the mini-boat 'Red Storm'. Scarborough High School is in Maine, one of the New England states on the eastern seaboard of the USA. The school has 995 pupils and their motto is 'Storm', hence the name of the vessel.

The students at this school developed a *"project that researches the effects of wind and current"*. A small, 56in (L) x 16in (W), (142cm x 41cm) unpowered boat with a keel and a small sail was built and fitted with a GPS transmitter to track its progress as it was carried by the wind and waves across the ocean.

'Red Storm' beached at Seaford Head
- Photo by Nikki Hills, SWT

'Red Storm' was launched in mid-Atlantic by the training ship 'The State of Maine', and after 98 days at sea was washed up on the foreshore of the Seaford Head Local Nature Reserve, the GPS pinpointing the exact position to the team tracking her progress. A transatlantic telephone call sent Nikki Hills, SWT's Learning and Engagement Officer racing down to the beach to find and retrieve the little craft which she plans to take into local schools to discuss the project with pupils before arranging for the re-launch of this plucky vessel.

What of the Future?

There is no doubt that the next fifty years will be equally, if not more, challenging than the last. Climate change wasn't recognised as an issue 50 years ago when Seaford Head teemed with wildlife some of which is probably already extinct and some having one of their last strongholds in the United Kingdom within the Reserve.

In common with all chalk cliffs on the south coast, Seaford Head is subject to the natural forces of erosion which mean that the Reserve will get smaller, as evidenced by three large collapses in 2017, fortunately just outside the Reserve.

The narrow strip of Reserve land right on the cliff edge will inevitably cease to exist, presenting unique challenges to the rare flora and fauna supported by this habitat and those who manage them.

Having signed a 25 year lease with the Sussex Wildlife Trust, the Seaford Town Council have ensured the Reserve is in safe hands and the land will continue to be safeguarded for the benefit of the public and the wildlife. Patrick McCausland

June 2017 cliff collapse
- *Image from Daily Telegraph*

and Tony Thorpe, both long standing members of the Management Committee, recalled that their darkest days were the withdrawal of the Ranger service when the Reserve became part of the Sussex Downs National Park and the Committee had no funds to continue their work; and their brightest days were when the SWT became involved and its future secured.

~ 50th Anniversary Event, Seaford Head, 13th July 2019 ~

Chairman, Chris Lowmass unveiling the Commemorative Plaque
~ Photos by Alison Baker

Above: Sarah Quantrill, SWT Ranger, leading a walk around the Reserve.
~ Photo courtesy Sussex Wildlife Trust

Above: 50th Anniversary Cake
~ Photo by Colin Pritchard, SNHS

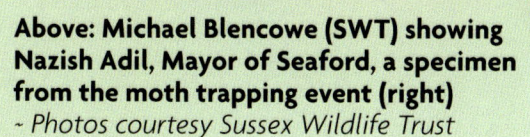

Above: Michael Blencowe (SWT) showing Nazish Adil, Mayor of Seaford, a specimen from the moth trapping event (right)
~ Photos courtesy Sussex Wildlife Trust

~ Appendices ~

Appendices

Appendix 1:

Seaford Head Local Nature Reserve Management Committee Chairs

1969 – 1971 =	Councillor V E Myers (Seaford Urban District Council)
1971 – 1972 =	Councillor S K White? (Seaford Urban District Council)
1972 – 1975 =	Councillor A W Heathcote (Seaford Urban District Council)
1975 – 1977 =	Councillor H Holmes (Lewes District Council)
1977 – 1991 =	Councillor Edward (Ted) Sales (Lewes District Council)
1991 – 1996 =	Cllr Kathleen W Amoore (Sussex Wildlife Trust) [also Secretary of the Seaford Natural History Society 1973 – 1996. 1996 was the year of her 90th birthday.]
1996 – 2004 =	Dr J P Rosser (Lewes District Council representative until 1999 then Seaford Town Council)
2004 – 2011 =	Mr Patrick McCausland (Sussex Wildlife Trust)
2011 – 2019 =	Mr Chris Lowmass (Sussex Ornithological Society)

Appendix 2:

Seaford Head Local Nature Reserve Rangers/Wardens (part-time)

1972 – 1974 =	B Lane (voluntary warden)
1974 – 1985 =	John Gascoigne
1985 – 1986 =	Michael Stagg
1986 – 1988 =	Monty Larkin with Richard (Dick) Mash
1988 – 1990 =	Monty Larkin with T Cox
1990 – 1991 =	Monty Larkin with S Manning
1986 – 1993 =	Monty Larkin
1993 – 1996 =	Paul Ling
1996 – 1999 =	Neil Featherstone
2000 – 2001 =	Fran Southgate

~ Appendices ~

Appendix2 (continued):

2001 – 2005 =   Simon McHugh
2005 - 2008 =   Tracey Younghusband
2008 – 2010 =   Alex Stephens/ Stephanie Diment
2010 – 2013 =   No Ranger service once South Downs National Park established
2013 – to date = Sarah Quantrill (Sussex Wildlife Trust)

Appendix 3:

Film Location

Seaford Head has been used as a location for numerous films, TV programmes, features and photographic shoots (an awful lot of adverts for cars!) during the last 50 years. There is documentary evidence in the Management Committee archives for the following:

1991 – 'Prince of Thieves', starring Kevin Costner
1995 – 'The Sculptress', TV drama starring Pauline Quirke
1995 – 'Jackanory' and 'Horizon', BBC programmes
1995 – 'Wall to Wall', documentary for Meridian TV
1995 – 'Hale and Pace', TV comedy show
1997 – An advertising shoot for Opel cars.
1999 – BBC remake of 'David Copperfield' by Charles Dickens
1999 – 'Lady Audley's Secret', starring Kenneth Cranham
2000 – 'The Bill', ITV series
2000 – 'Pearl Harbour', starring Ben Afflick and Kate Beckinsale
2004 – 'Harry Potter and the Goblet of Fire', starring Daniel Radcliffe
2007 – 'Atonement', starring Keira Knightley
2004 – 'Green Wing', Channel 4 TV series starring Stephen Mangan
2013 – Ellie Goulding for a music video,
2013 – 'Poirot', TV drama, for part of the last series.
2014 – 'Mr Holmes', starring Ian McKellen
2015 – 'Luther', BBC TV series starring Idris Elba
2018 – 'Hope Gap' starring Bill Nighy
2018 – 'Summerland' starring Gemma Arterton

~ Appendices ~

Appendix 4:

Species unique to Seaford Head among the 33 SWT-managed Nature Reserves (end of 2017 data)

Group	Species	Common Name	Date last seen
acarine (Acari)	*Aceria echii*	Aceria echii	2013
bird	*Anthus hodgsoni*	Olive-Backed Pipit	2003
bird	*Emberiza cirlus*	Cirl Bunting	1978
bird	*Ficedula parva*	Red-breasted Flycatcher	2009
bird	*Prunella collaris*	Alpine Accentor	1921
bird	*Sylvia nisoria*	Barred Warbler	2014
bird	*Tetrax tetrax*	Little Bustard	1846
flowering plant	*Diplotaxis tenuifolia*	Perennial Wall-rocket	2006
flowering plant	*Fallopia baldschuanica*	Russian Vine	2005
flowering plant	*Lepidium heterophyllum*	Smith's Pepperwort	2011
flowering plant	*Limonium binervosum*	Rock Sea-lavender	2015
flowering plant	*Seseli libanotis*	Moon Carrot	2015
fungus	*Calycina herbarum*	Calycina herbarum	2017
fungus	*Cystolepiota seminuda*	Bearded Dapperling	2017
fungus	*Entoloma pseudoturci*	Entoloma pseudoturci	2017
fungus	*Exidia repandana*	Birch Jelly	2017
fungus	*Hydropisphaera peziza*	Hydropisphaera peziza	2017
fungus	*Lepiota griseovirens*	Lepiota griseovirens	2017
fungus	*Lepiota subincarnata*	Fatal Dapperling	2017
fungus	*Patellaria atrata*	Patellaria atrata	2017
fungus	*Perenniporia ochroleuca*	Perenniporia ochroleuca	2017
fungus	*Puccinia malvacearum*	Mallow Rust	2017
fungus	*Sowerbyella radiculata*	Sowerbyella radiculata	2017
insect - beetle (Coleoptera)	*Anisodactylus poeciloides*	Saltmarsh Short-spur	2016
insect - beetle (Coleoptera)	*Cathormiocerus aristatus*	Trachyphloeus aristatus	2016
insect - beetle (Coleoptera)	*Longitarsus jacobaea*	Longitarsus jacobaea	2016
insect - beetle (Coleoptera)	*Philorhizus vectensis*	Philorhizus vectensis	2012

~ Appendices ~

Group	Species	Common Name	Date last seen
insect - beetle (Coleoptera)	*Trichosirocalus dawsoni*	Trichosirocalus dawsoni	2001
insect - beetle (Coleoptera)	*Trypocopris vernalis*	Spring Dumbledor	2014
insect - butterfly	*Lampides boeticus*	Long-tailed Blue	2013
insect - hymenopteran	*Andrena nigriceps*	Black-headed Mining Bee	2007
insect - hymenopteran	*Andrena niveata*	Long-fringed Mini-miner	2007
insect - hymenopteran	*Andrena pilipes*	Black Mining Bee	2008
insect - hymenopteran	*Anthophora retusa*	Potter Flower Bee	2016
insect - hymenopteran	*Bombus cullumanus*	Cullum's Bumble Bee	1923
insect - hymenopteran	*Didineis lunicornis*	Didineis lunicornis	2007
insect - hymenopteran	*Lestiphorus bicinctus*	Lestiphorus bicinctus	2007
insect - hymenopteran	*Macrophya punctumalbum*	Macrophya punctumalbum	2017
insect - hymenopteran	*Macrophya punctumalbum*	Privet Sawfly	2016
insect - hymenopteran	*Melecta albifrons*	Common Mourning Bee	2011
insect - moth	*Acronicta auricoma*	Scarce Dagger	1942
insect - moth	*Choreutis pariana*	Apple-leaf Skeletonizer	2015
insect - moth	*Coleophora versurella*	Pale Orache Case-bearer	2015
insect - moth	*Ectoedemia agrimoniae*	Agrimony Pigmy	2013
insect - moth	*Endothenia gentianaeana*	Teasel Marble	2013
insect - moth	*Epinotia subocellana*	White Sallow Bell	2015
insect - moth	*Idaea degeneraria*	Portland Ribbon Wave	2017
Insect - moth	*Mompha conturbatella*	Mompha conturbatella	2016
insect - moth	*Pyrausta ostrinalis*	Scarce Purple & Gold	2016
insect - moth	*Scrobipalpa instabilella*	Saltern Groundling	2015
insect - moth	*Teleiodes vulgella*	Common Groundling	2015
insect - moth	*Utetheisa pulchella*	Crimson Speckled	2013
insect - true bug (Hemiptera)	*Myzocallis schreiberi*	Myzocallis schreiberi	2014
insect - true bug (Hemiptera)	*Eurydema ornata*	Eurydema ornata	2015
insect - true fly (Diptera)	*Coenosia antennata*	Coenosia antennata	2016
insect - true fly (Diptera)	*Dolichopus pennatus*	Dolichopus pennatus	2016
insect - true fly (Diptera)	*Fannia similis*	Fannia similis	2016
insect - true fly (Diptera)	*Geranomyia unicolor*	Geranomyia unicolor	2016

~ Appendices ~

Group	Species	Common Name	Date last seen
insect - true fly (Diptera)	*Lamproscatella sibilans*	Lamproscatella sibilans	2016
insect - true fly (Diptera)	*Lucilia ampullacea*	Lucilia ampullacea	2016
insect - true fly (Diptera)	*Phora atra*	Phora atra	2016
insect - true fly (Diptera)	*Spilogona marina*	Spilogona marina	2016
insect - true fly (Diptera)	*Themira annulipes*	Themira annulipes	2016
insect - true fly (Diptera)	*Trimerana madizans*	Trimerana madizans	2016
lichen	*Agonimia gelatinosa*	Polyblastia gelatinosa	1994
lichen	*Bacidia bagliettoana*	Bacidia bagliettoana	1994
lichen	*Catapyrenium squamulosum*	Catapyrenium squamulosum	1994
lichen	*Cladonia convoluta*	Cladonia convoluta	1994
lichen	*Parmelia tiliacea*	Parmelia tiliacea	2016
lichen	*Physconia distorta*	Physconia distorta	1984
moss	*Bryum torquescens*	Twisting Thread-moss	2013

~ Bibliography ~

Bibliography

Bannister, N. R. (1999). *Chyngton Farm Historic Landscape Survey [for National Trust]*

Gordon, K, (2010), *A Seaford Timeline*

Kelly's Directory 1855, 1867, 1887 & 1891

Lewes District Council, Amenities Committee Minutes 1975 – 1980

Lewes District Council, Seaford sub-Committee Minutes 1979

Paul, D, archive material re 1932 Chyngton Estate sale

Portsmouth Evening News, 10th June 1927 accessed via the East Sussex Library Service

Seaford Head Local Nature Reserve Management Committee Minutes 1969 – 2018

Seaford Natural History Society Minutes 1960-2018

Seaford Museum and Heritage Society Archives

Seaford Town Council Archives

Seaford Urban District Council Minutes 1926-1933, 1953 & 1964-1970

Scarborough Public Schools: www.educationalpassages.org/boats/redstorm

Sussex Agricultural Express, various archive articles accessed via the East Sussex Library Service

Sussex Wildlife Trust

The Seaford Naturalist, newsletter of the SNHS, 1960-2019

The Times, various archive articles accessed via the East Sussex Library Service

Walsh, J. H. (1986). *Seaford Golf Club: A History*

www.ancestry.co.uk

www.artichoke.uk.com/project/peace-camp

www.britishnewspaperarchive.co.uk

www.telegraph.co.uk/news

www.google.co.uk

~ Glossary ~

Glossary

AGM	= Annual General Meeting
AONB	= Area of Outstanding Natural Beauty
BRC	= Biodiversity Record Centre
BTCV	= British Trust of Conservation Volunteers
BTO	= British Trust for Ornithology
CAA	= Civil Aviation Authority
CSS	= Countryside Stewardship Scheme
DEFRA	= Department for Environment, Food and Rural Affairs
EA	= Environment Agency
EN	= English Nature
ESA	= Environmentally Sensitive Area
ESCC	= East Sussex County Council
LDC	= Lewes District Council
LNR	= Local Nature Reserve
MAFF	= Ministry for Agriculture, Fisheries and Food
NCC	= Nature Conservancy Council
NE	= Natural England
NPA	= National Park Authority
NRA	= National Rivers Authority
NT	= National Trust
NVC	= National Vegetation Classification
RBL	= Royal British Legion
SDAONB	= South Downs Area of Outstanding Natural Beauty
SDCB	= Sussex Downs Conservation Board
SDJC	= South Downs Joint Committee
SDNPA	= South Downs National Park Authority
SDS	= South Downs Society (formerly Society of Sussex Downsmen)

~ Glossary ~

SHLNR	= Seaford Head Local Nature Reserve
SHLNRMC	= Seaford Head Local Nature Reserve Management Committee
SNHS	= Seaford Natural History Society
SDS	= South Downs Society
SOS	= Sussex Ornithological Society
SSSI	= Site of Special Scientific Interest
STC	= Seaford Town Council (1999 – present)
SUDC	= Seaford Urban District Council (1894 – 1974)
SWA	= Southern Water Authority
SWT	= Sussex Wildlife Trust
TIC	= Tourist Information Centre
VMCA	= Voluntary Marine Conservation Area

~ Index ~

A

Adder 79, 83
Adela croesella 78
Adil, Nazish 109
Aircraft navigation beacon 6, 7, 90, 91, 92, 93
Amoore, Kathleen 26, 77, 110
Ann, Michael 70
Anthophora retusa 15, 42, 77, 80, 82
Area of Outstanding Natural Beauty (AONB) 6, 20, 22, 92, 116
Artichoke Peace Camp 5, 86
Atonement 96, 111
Autumn Ladies Tresses 41, 84
Ayres, Mr J 96

B

Barber, Luke 106
Barred Tooth-striped Moth 79, 82
Batchelor, R (Bob) 7, 25
Beach 25, 42, 55, 56, 72
Beachy Head 9, 13, 60
Beetles 80
Bicycle parking rings 105
Biodiversity Action Plan 85
Biological Record Centre 79
Blatchington 11, 15, 73, 105
Blencowe, Michael 109
Bloody-nosed beetle 75
Brighton 8, 10, 16, 74, 94, 107
Brown, Cllr Bob 18, 39, 106
Buckle Church 63, 67
Bumble bees 75
Butterfly 26, 39, 75, 81, 84, 106
Butterfly Conservation Trust 84

C

Cable Hut 96, 97
Canadian Pond Weed 49
Canadian War Memorial 5, 7, 86, 87, 88, 89
Cattle-grazing 43
Chaffinch 85
Chalk sward 67

Chyngton Estate 11, 13, 33
Chyngton Farm 7, 20, 21, 22, 27, 29, 31, 33, 36, 52, 105
Cinnabar Moth 38
Civil Aviation Beacon (DVOR) 5, 7, 90, 91, 92, 93
Cladonia Convoluta 85
Coastal erosion 37, 39, 97
Coastguard Cottages 18, 20, 21, 22, 23, 31, 32, 34, 37, 53, 58, 67, 70, 86, 87, 95, 96, 97, 101, 106
Coleoptera 80, 112, 113
Comma butterfly 84
Commemorative Plaque 109
Commissioners of Crown Lands 99
Common Bird Census 41, 81, 82
Common Blue butterfly 39, 84
Common Carder Bee 76
Common European Viper 85
Common Lizard 33
Common Milkwort 43
Community Project Officer 43
Constitution 6, 19, 20, 21, 22, 23
Coppiced 33, 34, 35, 66, 67
Cotoneaster 42
Country Club 5, 94
Countryside Act 1949 6, 15, 17, 99
Countryside Commission 14, 20
County Ecologist 32, 66, 75, 76, 102
Cox, Mr T 45, 46, 62, 66
Crassula 49
Crickets 78
Crowlink Estate 13
Crown Estate Commissioners 99, 100
Cuckmere 7, 14, 15, 16, 17, 26, 31, 38, 42, 53, 58, 64, 68, 69, 70, 71, 72, 73, 74, 77, 86, 87, 88, 89, 96, 97, 98, 99, 100, 102, 103, 105, 106
Curson, Jon 37, 38, 70
Customs and Revenue Services 96

D

Daisy 78
Damselflies 78
Department for Environment, Food and Rural Affairs (DEFRA) 38, 116

~ Index ~

Diment, Stephanie 49, 111
Dewpond 5, 33, 45, 46, 47, 48, 49, 62
D L Paul & Sons Ltd 13, 19
Dogs 5, 32, 43, 50, 51, 53
Dor beetle 75
Dragonflies 78, 82
Drones 5, 95

E
Eade, Matt 41, 82
Earls of Chichester 10, 13
East Blatchington Pond Committee 105
Eastbourne 10, 16, 60, 107
East Sussex County Council 7, 14, 19, 20, 21, 22, 23, 32, 54, 58, 60, 72, 94, 116
Edwards, Leslie 87, 89
Emperor Moth 75
English Nature 22, 33, 34, 35, 37, 49, 64, 70, 76, 78, 79, 116
Entoloma pseudoturci 84, 112
Environment Agency (EA) 49, 69, 71, 72, 97, 116
Environmentally Sensitive Area (ESA) 7, 38, 116
Eurydema ornata 84, 113
Exceat 13, 14, 15, 73

F
Featherstone, Neil 21, 34, 48, 50, 55, 63, 67, 77, 78, 110
Ferrets 66, 67
Fiftieth anniversary 7, 9, 109
Filming 5, 96, 97
First species survey 73
Fisher, Len 57
Fletcher, Anne 8, 81
Fogle, Ben 97
Foreshore 5, 6, 7, 16, 18, 59, 85, 98, 99, 100, 101, 102, 107
Fulmar 95
Fungi 80, 84

G
Garbett, Mr C 67
Gascoigne, (A) John 6, 19, 20, 29, 32, 68, 102, 110

Gatekeeper butterfly 75, 84
Golden Galleon 53, 60, 63, 64
Golf course 6, 10, 11, 12, 22, 31, 36, 37, 39, 41, 42, 56, 78, 85
Governance 5, 19, 20, 21, 22, 23, 24, 25, 26, 27, 28, 31, 43, 57, 80, 97
Grasshoppers 78
Grass snake 79, 83
Great green bush cricket 78
Greenwing 97
Green-winged Orchid 77, 84

H
Harison, Launcelot 10
Harrison, H J 7, 16, 17, 25
Harry's Bush 5, 7, 17, 18, 23, 32, 40, 52, 53
Harvey, DH 16, 25, 29
Hayward, Mr T 20
Heathcote AW (John) 26, 110
Helicella itala 80
Hemingway, GEC (Chris) 7, 15, 16, 26, 28, 30, 59, 69, 73, 74, 75, 76
Heritage Coast 6, 9, 56, 69, 77
Heritage Lottery Fund 24, 43
Heteroptera 80
Hills, Nikki 24, 44, 107
Holmes, Mr H 110
Hooper, Cllr James 12
Hope Gap 5, 7, 15, 28, 29, 31, 33, 34, 35, 37, 41, 42, 54, 55, 56, 57, 58, 62, 63, 66, 67, 69, 72, 74, 77, 79, 80, 81, 95, 96, 98, 99, 103, 106, 107, 111
Hope Gap Steps 5, 37, 42, 54, 55, 56, 57, 58, 63, 72, 95
Howell, Jim 98
Hutchings, Alfred Blandford 11

I
ILoveSeaford app 61
Interact Club of Seaford 28
Interpretation Boards 5, 62, 63, 64
Iron Age camp 104

~ Index ~

J

Juvenile Common Shrew 81

L

Ladies Tresses 41, 84
Land Acquisition 5, 10, 11, 12, 13, 14, 96
Land Management 5, 20, 23, 28, 29, 30, 31, 32, 33, 34, 35, 36, 37, 38, 39, 40, 41, 42, 43, 44, 74
Lane, Mr B 110
Large Skipper butterfly 84
Larkin, Monty 20, 32, 53, 55, 69, 97, 104, 110
Leaflets 6, 46, 59, 60, 61
Leisure Services Committee 46, 66, 98, 99, 100
Lepidoptera 78
Lepiota cf. andegavensis 84
Lewes District Council (LDC) 6, 7, 8, 12, 14, 17, 19, 20, 21, 22, 23, 26, 27, 38, 45, 46, 47, 50, 53, 54, 55, 56, 57, 58, 60, 64, 66, 67, 68, 80, 90, 91, 92, 94, 95, 97, 98, 99, 100, 102, 103, 104, 105, 110, 115, 116
Lewes District Councillors 21
Lichen 85, 114
Ling, Paul 20, 33, 47, 48, 50, 63, 77, 110
Little Bustard 85, 112
Lizards 85
Local Geological Site 9
Local Government Reform Act 1974 6, 14, 19
Local Nature Reserve (LNR) 3, 5, 6, 7, 8, 9, 14, 15, 16, 17, 18, 19, 22, 26, 28, 31, 46, 54, 69, 70, 73, 79, 86, 91, 94, 96, 99, 100, 101, 104, 107, 110, 116
Lowmass, Chris 9, 26, 41, 75, 106, 109, 110
Lullington Close 31, 36, 37, 39, 76
Lyons, Graeme 23, 40, 61, 82, 83, 85

M

McCausland, Patrick 27, 38, 108, 110
McCourt, Carolyn 87
McHugh, Simon 22, 36, 37, 38, 49, 64, 70, 97, 106

Management Committee 3, 6, 7, 8, 9, 16, 19, 20, 21, 22, 23, 25, 26, 27, 28, 29, 32, 33, 34, 37, 39, 40, 41, 42, 43, 45, 46, 47, 50, 51, 52, 54, 55, 56, 57, 59, 61, 62, 64, 65, 66, 67, 68, 69, 70, 71, 72, 74, 75, 76, 77, 78, 80, 82, 83, 86, 87, 89, 90, 92, 93, 94, 95, 97, 98, 99, 100, 102, 104, 105, 108, 110, 111, 115, 117
Management Plan 7, 22, 23, 25, 28, 29, 30, 31, 34, 35, 38, 39, 40, 41, 45, 46, 49, 61, 70, 74, 77, 78, 80, 81
Martello Tower Local History Museum 12, 100
Masters, Tom 36
Ministry for Agriculture, Fisheries and Food (MAFF) 98, 116
Molluscs 98
Moon Carrot 15, 28, 41, 77, 81, 82, 83, 112
Moths 75, 78, 82
Myers, V E (Vic) 19, 110

N

National Park 6, 7, 9, 22, 23, 38, 39, 41, 42, 57, 61, 71, 72, 108, 111, 116
National Trust 7, 8, 13, 14, 20, 21, 22, 23, 27, 33, 60, 63, 72, 77, 82, 85, 95, 116
National Vegetation Classification 76, 78, 116
Natural England 7, 16, 19, 22, 23, 25, 40, 41, 67, 71, 86, 93, 116
Natural History Society 7, 8, 15, 16, 17, 19, 20, 21, 22, 23, 26, 28, 29, 30, 41, 42, 47, 65, 69, 73, 74, 75, 76, 77, 79, 81, 82, 83, 84, 85, 95, 110, 115, 117
Nature Conservancy 15, 16, 17, 18, 19, 25, 28, 29, 68, 94, 101, 116
Nature Conservancy Council 17, 18, 68, 94, 101, 116
Nature Reserve 3, 5, 6, 7, 8, 9, 14, 15, 16, 17, 18, 19, 22, 25, 26, 28, 31, 44, 46, 53, 54, 61, 69, 70, 73, 74, 75, 76, 81, 83, 86, 91, 94, 96, 98, 99, 100, 104, 107, 110, 112, 115, 116, 117
Nesting 17, 42, 52, 53, 91, 95, 104
Newhaven 9, 16, 97, 106
Northcote, Hugh Hamilton Stafford 6, 13

O

Oak Eggar Moth Caterpillar 43
Odonata 78
Oeters, Renee 54

~ Index ~

Oil Pollution 5, 102, 103
One-offs 5, 55, 104, 105, 106, 107
Open Days 5, 65
Orchid 77, 84
Ornate Shieldbug 83, 84
Orthoptera 78
Ortolan Buntings 74

P

Parrots Feather 48, 49
Pathfinder 70, 71
Paul, Daniel 13
Paul, David W 13, 19, 20, 21, 22, 27, 29
Peace Camp 5, 86
Perenniporia ochroleuca 84, 112
Periwinkles 98
Philanthus triangulum 77
Phillips, Andy 40
Plant Bugs 80
Port, Martin 16, 74
Potter Flower-bee 15, 42, 77, 80, 82
Praise Plaque 55, 105
Promotion 5, 59, 60, 61
Publicity 59, 60, 61
Public rights of way 40

Q

Quantrill, Sarah 23, 24, 40, 41, 42, 43, 44, 51, 72, 107, 109, 111

R

Rabbits 5, 35, 66, 67, 77, 78
Ranger 19, 20, 21, 22, 23, 24, 25, 32, 33, 34, 35, 36, 37, 38, 39, 40, 41, 43, 44, 45, 47, 48, 49, 50, 51, 53, 55, 56, 62, 63, 64, 65, 66, 67, 69, 70, 72, 77, 79, 80, 97, 104, 106, 108, 109
Readers Digest Beachwatch 69, 77
Red Admiral butterfly 84
Red Data Book 77, 79, 85
Red Kites 106
Red Storm 107
Regionally Important Geomorphological Site 9
Reptiles 82

Robin 80
Rosser, Jill 21, 110
Roosting 17, 52
Round-headed Rampion 73
Royal British Legion (RBL) 87, 88, 116
Russian Vineweed 42, 43

S

Sales, E L (Ted) 20, 26, 47, 110
Saline Lagoon 5, 42, 43, 68, 69, 70, 71, 72
Saltmarsh 40, 42, 71
South Downs Joint Committee (SDJC) 22, 23, 116
Seaford Bay 99, 102
Seaford Community Wildlife Project 24
Seaford Head 3, 5, 6, 7, 8, 9, 11, 12, 13, 14, 15, 16, 17, 19, 21, 22, 29, 31, 34, 39, 41, 44, 46, 54, 57, 61, 73, 74, 75, 76, 85, 90, 94, 96, 99, 102, 104, 105, 106, 107, 108, 109, 110, 111, 112, 115, 116, 117
Seaford Head Local Nature Reserve Management Committee (SHLNRMC) 5, 6, 8, 9, 16, 19, 59, 60, 70, 94, 104, 110, 115, 117
Seaford Lifeguards 106
Seaford Natural History Society 7, 8, 17, 19, 20, 21, 22, 23, 26, 29, 69, 74, 76, 79, 85, 110, 115, 117
Seaford Town Council (STC) 7, 8, 14, 18, 21, 22, 23, 30, 33, 34, 36, 38, 39, 40, 43, 46, 47, 51, 53, 57, 58, 61, 73, 74, 90, 91, 92, 97, 100, 101, 108, 110, 115, 117
Seaford Urban District Council (SUDC) 6, 12, 13, 14, 16, 17, 19, 26, 28, 54, 90, 99, 110, 115, 117
Seseli libanotis 81, 112
Seven Sisters 14, 17, 19, 29, 59, 60, 63, 96, 97
Sheep 32, 37, 41, 42, 43, 46
Shellfish 98, 99, 100
Site of Nature Conservation Importance 9
Site of Special Scientific Interest (SSSI) 6, 7, 9, 15, 17, 18, 86, 95, 117
Slow worms 83
Small Copper butterfly 84
Small Heath butterfly 84
Small Skipper butterfly 84

~ Index ~

Smelt, Mr R 96
Society of Sussex Downsmen 21, 22, 23, 26, 37, 116
Sole, Peter 66
South Downs 6, 7, 14, 21, 22, 26, 39, 42, 47, 57, 59, 61, 64, 70, 71, 72, 76, 80, 81, 92, 111, 116, 117
South Downs National Park (SDNP) 6, 7, 39, 42, 43, 57, 61, 71, 72, 111, 116
Southern Water Authority (SWA) 68, 69, 102, 103, 117
Southgate, Fran 21, 22, 35, 56, 65, 79, 110
South Hill Barn 13, 16, 31, 32, 33, 39, 45, 46, 47, 48, 49, 50, 56, 57, 63, 64, 80, 104, 105
South Hill Farm 13
Sowerbyella radiculata 84, 112
Splash Point 58
Stagg, Michael 32, 110
Stephens, Alex 39, 64, 111
Stone Crop 49
Sussex Biodiversity Record Centre 83, 85
Sussex Downs Conservation Board (SDCB) 20, 22, 46, 57, 62, 69, 77, 97, 116
Sussex Fish Survey 81
Sussex Fungi Group 84
Sussex Naturalists Trust 7, 16, 19, 25, 28
Sussex Ornithological Society 7, 19, 20, 21, 23, 25, 26, 78, 81, 104, 110, 117
Sussex Species Action Plan 80
Sussex Wildlife Trust (SWT) 5, 7, 8, 16, 19, 21, 23, 24, 25, 26, 27, 28, 39, 40, 42, 43, 49, 53, 61, 71, 72, 81, 82, 83, 84, 85, 95, 97, 107, 108, 109, 110, 111, 112, 115, 117
Sustrans Cycle Route 105
Sutton Estate 10, 11
Sutton Place 10, 11

T
Tawny Pipit 74
Terms of Reference 6, 21

The Buckle 100
The Keep 8, 45, 94
The Seaford Naturalist 17, 76, 77, 115
The Sisterhood of Mary 105
Thorpe, Tony 26, 64, 108
Tourist Information Centres 59, 60
Town and Country Planning Act 94
Town Seal of Seaford 10
Trichopteryx polycommata 79
Twayblade 84

U
User Survey 57

V
Vanguard Way 9, 31, 106
Vestal Cuckoo Bee 36
Voluntary Marine Conservation Area 7, 9, 117
Volunteers 21, 23, 24, 25, 29, 35, 41, 42, 43, 44, 48, 49, 69, 70, 72, 74, 75, 77, 79, 84

W
Wader Pool 68
Wallraven, Cllr Linda 24
Wasps 76, 77
Wasp Spider 35
Wheatears 104
White, Cllr S K 51, 110
Whiteman, Colin 82, 83, 95
Wild Mink 104
Wild privet 35, 67
Winged orchid 77
World War I 6, 106

Y
Yellow-footed Mining bee 85
Yellowhammer 85
Younghusband, Tracey 22, 38, 39, 51, 64, 67, 80, 111